PROGRAM FULL:

Your Guide to Successful Childcare Marketing

PROGRAM FULL:

YOUR GUIDE TO SUCCESSFUL CHILDCARE MARKETING

Taffy Gallagher

iUniverse, Inc.

New York   Bloomington

Program Full
Your Guide To Successful Childcare Marketing

iUniverse books may be ordered through booksellers or by contacting:

iUniverse
1663 Liberty Drive
Bloomington, IN 47403
www.iuniverse.com
1-800-Authors (1-800-288-4677)

ISBN: 978-1-4401-9680-5 (pbk)
ISBN: 978-1-4401-9952-3 (ebook)

Designed by Taffy Gallagher
SECOND EDITION

Printed in the United States of America

iUniverse rev. date: 12/29/09

DISCLAIMER

The content of this book is meant to provide information to help you promote and market your childcare business. We encourage you to read other material on the same subject to learn more about marketing and promotions. Many of the ideas presented in this book may require expert assistance. We strongly recommend that you seek assistance in the appropriate professional service field. The author and publisher of this text shall not be held responsible to any person or entity regarding any loss or damage caused (or alleged to have been caused) directly or indirectly by the information in this book.

To Aaron

Special thank you to:
Mom and Papa
Amber Havens and Educational Training Partners
Cody
Shannon Schinagl, Karin Watson
Courtney Huber, Sally Smith, Wanda Selg Gonzales
Michelle Kuwasaki and Barbara Culler
Jennifer Crossen, Bonnie Duncan, Jeffrey Thomas

CONTENTS

CONTENTS

Chapter One

First Steps

INTRODUCTION

This book is based on a popular workshop I developed exclusively for the childcare industry. The workshop is never long enough to fully convey the information participants seek. So I began writing extended guidance for the most requested topics, which became the foundation for this book.

My intention was to create a book that does more than tell you what to do to market your childcare business. I want you to gain the confidence to apply what you learn and extend that knowledge to marketing efforts you dream up on your own. You will find practical tips, solutions and ideas that guide you with relevant examples and hands-on activities to help you implement your own marketing campaign.

The following pages are written specifically for owners, directors, assistant directors, board members of childcare and early learning facilities, family childcare businesses and anyone responsible for keeping enrollment up in their center, including non-profit and for-profit programs. This book is also for anyone about to open the doors of their new childcare business, anyone who has been in business for any length of time or anyone thinking about starting his or her own childcare business. Use the book to familiarize yourself with the basics of marketing and how it relates to your responsibilities as a childcare professional.

You might be surprised to learn that you were engaging in marketing long before you opened the doors to your center. In the next chapter, you will realize how much marketing you have already done. For now, take inventory of your personal capabilities. Business owners and leaders must have a certain set of attributes to engage in successful marketing. Ambition, a positive attitude, an open mind, passion for your business or career, and the willingness to take a risk are traits that contribute to success. Although marketing can be scary at times, it can be elating at others, so you must have patience too.

A few tools that are helpful to have, but are not always necessary, are: access to a computer, access to the Internet, word processing software (Microsoft® Word or WordPerfect), web publishing software (FrontPage®, GoLive®, Dreamweaver®), desktop publishing software (Publisher®, Illustrator®, InDesign®, Freehand®) and photo editing software (Photoshop®, Paint Shop Pro®). Check with your local library for access to some of these programs.

Are you excited about the responsibility of marketing or would you rather be training faculty, working in the classroom or balancing your accounts? This book helps take the mystery out of marketing and assists you in creating a plan for your center or program that you can follow for a year without changing anything, allowing you to focus on other aspects of your career or business.

Others of you might find excitement in this element of your responsibilities. Use this book as a springboard to more advanced marketing activities. You will find good ideas and activities that help the creative juices start flowing. Once you have reached the limits of what Program Full can do for you, use the resources (Appendix A) to expand your knowledge. Visit the library for books on design and copy writing. Take a course in design or photography to enhance your skills. Join a networking group for childcare administration and make sure marketing is on the discussion list.

There is no single right or wrong plan for any business, but in order to see results, you need to recognize and accept four rules:

You must COMMIT to your marketing plan and not waver.

You must provide CONSISTENCY among all marketing efforts.

You must regard marketing as a long-term INVESTMENT.

You must have PATIENCE.

Commitment: Marketing requires a long-term commitment. You must commit yourself to your plan for eight to twelve months before you can truly determine if a specific effort is working. It takes several months of marketing to see any results and many more months of *effective* marketing to see positive results. Make a pledge to never drift from your marketing plan until you know the results of your efforts.

Consistency: The key to successful marketing is consistency. Staying consistent with your color and typeface (font) selection, logo usage, message and the methods you select to employ create a sense of permanency and reassurance amid faculty, customers, potential customers and the community.

Investment: Marketing rarely pays you back immediately. Give your plan time to see the financial results of your marketing efforts for two reasons: 1) because people are slow to respond to marketing and advertising and 2) because you must reinvest income in your marketing to ensure consistency. Over the long run, if you adhere to these four rules, your investment should begin offering a return.

Patience: Results from your marketing activities take time to reveal themselves. You might get immediate response, but most often it takes a combination of these four rules to reap the benefits of marketing. If you become frustrated by the amount of time and money it takes to see results, focus on the marketing that costs you little or nothing. It will not only keep you focused on your plan, but will help to improve the results that are on their way. (See Chapters 4 and 6 for cost-effective marketing tips.)

WHY SHOULD YOU MARKET?

- It keeps your existing customers from leaving your center for another one.

- Your competition is marketing and acquiring your prospective families.

- Your market is always changing. People move in and out of your geographical target area daily and new centers open up nearby each month.

- People have a tendency to forget. This means that you have to continue marketing with unfailing consistency.

- It supports confidence among faculty, customers, and potential customers.

HOW TO USE THIS BOOK

Terminology

For the purpose of clear communication, the terminology used to represent various aspects of business in the childcare industry should be clarified, as they are used interchangeably throughout this book. I recently encountered a group of leaders in the industry who discussed how they could help change thoughts and perceptions by simply adjusting the terminology they use. The topic was the terms staff vs. faculty. They shared experiences regarding perception based on the two different words used. The conclusion was that the term faculty communicated teacher and staff expressed the idea of a worker and service provider. Also, while some of you may refer to yourself as daycares and childcare centers, others call themselves preschools, educational centers, or early learning centers, leading people to make assumptions about what you do. Common perception is that teachers and faculty <u>educate</u> young children and caregivers <u>care</u> for young children. Most of you, however, do both. So, what do you call yourself? How do you introduce yourself and your colleagues?

This book does not solve dilemmas with the terminology. It simply points out that there are various thoughts on the matter and because this book is for everyone in the industry, the terms are interchanged throughout the text.

Often, several terms are used to describe a single person or

The competition

Your competition consists of any business or organization that provides childcare services in your area or wherever your families travel to work. For example, the center six blocks away is a competitor, just like the one next door to one of the parent's place of employment.

Knowing who your competition is, what their services are and how they are marketing to your prospects and current customers is essential to your strategy. You need to have a healthy understanding of which centers you are competing with to create an effective marketing plan.

However, I do not promote an unhealthy concentration on profit, using misleading language to promote your center or speaking ill of the competition to place your business in a better light. Not only are these activities in poor taste, they often have the opposite effect and you end up losing credibility within the community.

concept. For example, the purchaser of your services will most often be called a customer, client, patron, parent, caregiver or family. Potential customers are also referred to as prospects. Your place of business is called a center, program, business or organization, but refers to all of the following: family childcare, General Services Administration (GSA) childcare, center-based care, co-op preschools, non-profit childcare and other types of childcare not listed here. A marketing effort is also called a campaign or an activity. Written text is sometimes called copy: web copy, brochure copy, advertising copy, etc.

Activities

Several activities are provided to help you gain a deeper understanding of what marketing is and how to begin thinking like a marketer. Completion of these activities is up to you, but for optimum retention and application of the concepts introduced throughout the following pages, it is advisable to work through them as they are presented in each chapter. Take full advantage of this book by avoiding the temptation to look ahead. Each chapter builds on the knowledge of the previous ones, making it more difficult to understand or complete the activities in the later chapters if you have not read the beginning.

> *When was the last time you were marketed to? How did the company or organization market to you?*
>
> *What was the last thing you purchased based on its marketing? Did the final product or service meet your expectations?*

Ideas notebook

I recommend keeping a notebook for inspirational moments. Create a habit of carrying a pen and small notebook with you for times when you think of a marketing idea that you want to explore. These ideas can strike anywhere; so, keep one by the bed, in your purse, at your desk, near the television, and in other places you spend time.

What if your program is full?

Although this situation is less common and the question appears to have a simple answer, it is still an important point to address. The quick answer is that you should never stop marketing. You have no control over the lives of the families you serve. Someone could lose a job, move out of the area, get in an accident, win the lottery, etc.

You should continue marketing to keep the momentum going. If you are consistently marketing, a promotion for anticipated slumps (or one for unexpected loss of students) is more likely to produce desired results. Imagine all of the work if you had to start from scratch each time you need to fill an opening.

Once you have a good plan and your program has a waiting list, you will have figured out what works for you. All you have to do is maintain it. Maintaining a successful marketing plan is far easier than creating a new one.

Why did you buy this book?

Is your business slow? Do you anticipate shifting enrollment? Is your competition increasing? Do you have a general curiosity about marketing in the childcare industry? Whatever your reason, the next step is to become familiar with what marketing is and how you can begin using it effectively.

Marketing does not often deliver immediate and grand results, and simply reading this book will not make you an expert on all marketing concepts. It does, however, provide you with tips and guidelines for improving the effectiveness of your marketing. When you have finished reading it, you will be inspired to try something you never thought about before or something you did not think you could do. The book also introduces more techniques to study and skills to develop. Use it as a guide when you are in the middle of a marketing project or as inspiration when you set aside time to plan your strategy.

By understanding the scope of marketing, setting a budget, making a plan, sticking to your plan, measuring the results and adjusting the plan accordingly, you will find that engaging in marketing is a never-ending process that can be thrilling as well as rewarding. It is a long process that requires commitment, consistency, investment, and patience.

WHAT EXACTLY IS MARKETING?

To answer this question, let's ask ourselves what marketing is not and then maybe we can better understand what it <u>is</u>. Most people might say that accounting does not interact with marketing, except for setting the marketing budget. That may seem true, but from the marketer's point of view every part of accounting is marketing related. Whether you pay your bills on time or 60 days late communicates something about you and your business to the vendor.

Perception matters

The quality of the envelope you use to pay your bills, how fast your payment is received and whether you make full or partial payments can all be considered marketing. Each one has the ability to influence personal opinion and therefore word-of-mouth. Let's say you rarely pay your grocery bill in full or on time. What is the person managing your account going to think about the type of business you run? Think about how you and your teachers present yourselves on a field trip. Has anyone worn something inappropriate or acted in way that did not represent your program with the message you want? Many people do not consider these types of business activities to be marketing, but if it makes an impression on anyone (either good or bad), it is marketing.

While these examples and more can be considered marketing, they are not entirely what this book is about. We are concerned with active and direct marketing to increase the level of sales activity at your center: more phone calls, more visitors, more enrollments.

Marketing is everything you do (and how you do it) that has the potential to influence the perception people have of your program.

ACTIVITY A

How many things can you think of that can be considered marketing? Take out some paper and spend five minutes listing every marketing method you can think of, such as: web site, brochure and yellow pages advertisement. When you have exhausted your knowledge bank, turn the page for a long (but not complete) list. Compare your ideas of what marketing is to this list and take note of those items you may not have listed. Did you come up with any that are not on the following list?

A new brochure meets its goal

Lowering the number of incoming telephone calls is not necessarily a goal most businesses seek. However, for one preschool, that was exactly what they wanted their new brochure to help them accomplish. They hoped that by referring interested parents to their web site and offering a map to their location the result would be fewer daily phone call interruptions — and they were correct.

To keep costs down, they decided on a three-panel brochure set up on 8.5" x 11" 24# white paper and designed with two colors. (When folded, it fits into a standard business envelope.) White paper was selected because the school sometimes displays their brochure on a table next to the brochures of other programs in the community, which are printed predominately with black ink on colored paper. The effect was an eye-catching bright white brochure that stood out among the sea of orange, purple, yellow, blue, pink, and lime papers.

The brochure organized relevant information on each panel and included items such as: their logo, web address in three or four locations, a welcome message from the director, basic information on the teachers and a map to their location. The school's Web address is referenced in several areas, directing people to the site. However, this also created the need to keep their site updated, which has proved to be a successful form of communication for this school. Since pricing changes annually, the director also created a pricing insert that fits inside the folded brochure, giving the brochure a much longer shelf life.

Not only did more people pick up the brochure, but they visited the preschool's web site to answer their questions BEFORE calling to make an appointment to visit. The brochure was a success!

ACTIVITY A: Methods

Advertising – Classified	*Direct Mail*
Advertising – Grocery Cart	*Door Hangers*
Advertising – Magazine	*Dress Code*
Advertising – Movie Screen	*Dry Cleaner Hangers*
Advertising – Newspaper	*Educational Directory*
Advertising – Radio	*Email*
Advertising – Search Engines	*Envelopes*
Advertising – Television	*Flyers*
Balloons	*Fundraiser*
Banners	*Good Reputation*
Billboards	*Hats*
Body Language	*Hired Clown (on street/corner)*
Bookmarks	*Hosted Events*
Booth at Fair or Carnival	*Hours of Operation*
Brochures	*Letterhead*
Business Cards	*Letters*
Canvassing	*Location*
Center Cleanliness	*Logo*
Center Orderliness	*Magnets*
Community Bulletin Board	*Mouse Pads*
Community Events	*Networking*
Cost of Service	*News (TV, Newspaper)*
Coupons	*Newsletters*
Curb Appeal	*Open House*
Customer Service	*Parade*

Pens	*Size of Center*
Personal Hygiene	*Sponsorship (Team, Event)*
Phone book – White Pages	*Staff Knowledge*
Phone book – Yellow Pages	*Stickers*
Postcards	*Tattoos (stick on)*
Posters	*Tear-off Flyers*
Post-Its (Preprinted program info.)	*Telemarketing*
Preschool Fair	*Telephone Etiquette*
Presentations	*Thank You Cards*
Press Releases	*Tone of Voice*
Reader Boards	*T-shirts*
Referral Program	*Vehicle/Auto Signs*
Resource & Referral Agencies	*Water Bottles*
Services Offered	*Web site*
Signs	*Welcome Package*
Silent Auction	*Word-of-Mouth*

ACTIVITY B

You now understand a little more about the many shapes marketing can take. It is your location, your tone of voice, and the cost of your service. It is also the quality (or existence) of your business card, your parent relations and the smile on your face when parents arrive to pick up their children.

Let's look at reasons to market or what the main message of the campaign is. In other words, what can you think of that gives you an excuse to market? Make a list of reasons you could use any of the items in Activity A to promote your business, such as: NAEYC Accreditation or the anniversary of your center.

ACTIVITY B: Reasons to market

This is a good list, but definitely not a complete one. If you are looking for more ideas, use the list from Activity A for inspiration.

Anniversary

Celebrating 5 years in business! Celebrating 20 years in business!

Carnival

Offer fun activities, vendors and food for families, community members and faculty

Child Development Associate (CDA) Certificate Earned

Congratulations to _____name_____ for earning their CDA

Change in Service

Now available: before and after school care. New early bird hours: now open at 6:00 AM

Charity Event

Warm clothes drive, sponsored by your center

Holidays*
Introducing the Center

Welcome to our neighborhood!

NAEYC Accreditation

We did it! (Explain how NAEYC Accreditation benefits children, families and staff.)

New Payment Options

Credit cards now accepted

New Faculty Member

Welcome Teacher Emily to the Eagle Classroom.

Open House

Meet your child's teachers and classmates.

Partnership

Teamed with local Senior Center — offer activities that bring young and old together

Questionnaire

Let us know how we are doing

Referral Program

Free day of service for each referred family who enrolls a student

Seasonal

Back to School or Winter Freeze – Get out of the cold with our hot savings!

Special Promotion

One week free! (with three months paid in full)

Sponsorship

Offer space/classrooms for CPR classes, babysitting classes, etc.

Training Obtained

All staff attended state conference and learned about...

Unique Event

Mud Day (Children are allowed to explore in a prepared area of mud)

* Be sensitive when promoting and celebrating holidays or other cultural events. Try not to offend the original event with literal interpretations of culture. To avoid stereotyping and misrepresentation, make the materials and event culturally appropriate and any activities developmentally relevant. For more information on this subject, read <u>Celebrate!: An Anti-Bias Guide to Enjoying Holidays in Early Childhood Programs</u> by Julie Bisson.

Chapter Two

Marketing Methods

Now that you have learned that marketing is more than your brochure and outdoor sign, you are probably wondering what to do next. A sensible first step is to identify your strengths, as well as obstacles you face that need creative solutions. You can then focus on developing campaigns to implement quickly, as well as identifying solutions that require more time to execute.

Let's say that you have a fantastic faculty, excellent location, and very little money to spend. A good plan for you would be to focus on your faculty–keep them happy and encourage their professional development. The secondary focus could be to use your location to promote your center like never before. Draw attention to yourself: put up a large sign, paint your building with vibrant colors and/or a mural that sets it apart from its environment (get permission first, of course), get an A-board/sandwich board for the sidewalk and put out fresh balloons weekly, take the kids outside on field trips each week with t-shirts advertising your center, partner with another local business to promote your great locations, offer your conveniently located classrooms for events and make sure you tell the community about it with your own marketing, as well as in the event organizer's promotional materials.

ACTIVITY C

Assess the strengths of your program and obstacles that need creative solutions by making a two-column list like below. Depending on your current and unique situation, obstacles on this list may be seen as strengths to others and vice versa.

Strengths	Obstacles
Excellent location	Small budget
Highly-qualified faculty	Few software skills
Large classrooms	Part-time program
NAEYC or other Accreditation	Preschool only (no infants or school-age)
Good relationships with families	Lack of cooking facilities (no prepared meals)
Transportation vehicles	
Consistent positive feedback from parents	

By understanding your strengths and obstacles, you can either find a way to make the obstacles strengths or adjust your communication regarding the obstacles to create a benefit to families. For example: You can add the service of extended hours to a part time program and promote the new service as a strength. OR, you can change the way you look at an obstacle and communicate it as a benefit to families. If you do not provide prepared lunches, you can say: "You don't have to worry about the food we're feeding her. Since you prepare her lunch, you know what your child is eating." As you can see, there are really very few obstacles. How you decide to approach each one can turn them into strengths. A small business should explore all tools and methods available, especially those that use strengths effectively. So, let's look closer at some of those methods.

The key for small businesses is to get directly in front of your potential customers. Where are they and how can you best reach them? The target market is different for every program, so read on to determine which ones best meet your needs.

Client relations

Practicing excellent customer service is one of the most cost effective means of marketing. You have the opportunity to make an impression on your customers every single day, an opportunity other types of businesses would pay for. Use it to your advantage by training faculty to represent your program with concern for your families' experiences. Happy customers tell others about their positive experiences, but they also spread the word about bad experiences. In fact, it is more likely that they will talk about their bad feelings and experiences before they talk about their good ones. Although the process can take longer, you will spend less money getting your current customers to keep their children enrolled in your center while referring others to you than you would trying to find prospects and market directly to them.

Competitive research

Know who your competition is, what services they offer, what their strengths and obstacles are, and what differentiates your program from each of them. If your competition offers services your families need that you do not offer, you are likely to see business shift from your center to one down the street.

To help you stay competitive consider: expanding your service hours, providing lunches, or offering flexible schedules that include drop-in care or sick care, etc.

Assessing the competition
- Create a matrix to track what you want to know (see next page for example) and start sleuthing to fill in the blanks.
- Begin on the Web. You can obtain information about a company on their web site or by searching your local newspaper online.
- Check the phone book for ads. See what they are advertising.
- Stop by or call for some basic information on services and costs.

School/Program	Services & Hours	Differentiators	Notes
Name and address or general location.	*What are their basic services and hours of operation?*	*What do they do differently or better? Is it something you could do?*	*Might you partner with them for an event or referrals?*

Media

The best way to obtain the attention of your local paper is to identify something newsworthy about your center and invite them to write an article. You can send a press release or call them directly, just make sure you communicate your idea clearly and are prepared to answer their questions concerning the value of your news idea. Remember that they want to write stories, but they will say no if they do not see an important or relevant message for their readers.

If you cannot identify an existing story, generate an event that is deserving of media coverage. MudDay is a good example. Obtain proper permission from parents and create a muddy play area for your students. Inform parents and the reporter of the reasons this type of play and exploration are valuable, and invite both to attend.

A story you think is valuable may not always top the list for a reporter, especially during times of other big news.

There are hundreds of books on this subject that walk you through various levels of gaining media coverage, from writing a press release to developing an extensive campaign. Two of them are listed in Appendix A. If you are interested in taking advantage of this highly effective marketing method, do your homework and get creative!

Surveys / Questionnaires

If you do not offer the services your clients need, they may go somewhere else. Sometimes, simply asking people what they think promotes positive customer relations. If you implement any of their suggested changes, your customers will likely become very satisfied. For example, if you find that a majority of parents want teachers to communicate more with them about daily activities of the children, work with your staff to devise several alternatives to meeting the parents' request. Construct a plan for teachers to put into action and ask parents about it again in three or four months.

You may want to ask:

- Are you generally satisfied with the level of service and quality of care and education at our center?
- Do you feel that your child is getting appropriate care and guidance at our center?
- Is there any particular area that you would like to see improvement in?

Allow parents to stay anonymous by not asking for their name and leaving a drop box for completed surveys in your entry hall.

You will certainly have more specific questions to which you want answers, but try to be brief. A half or full-page questionnaire with four to six questions is about right. If you're having trouble writing the questions, there are various places on the Web that offer advice on what to ask and how to word your questions.

Partnerships

A partnership is often a smart way to join forces (and bank accounts) with another business or organization trying to promote their product or service. Depending on the arrangement and your goals, you can effectively create an entire campaign surrounding the relationship. For example, you can partner with the business next door to share the costs of designing, printing and mailing a postcard. Or, you can partner with a local Senior Center to share those same costs, but your long-term plan is much different: Maybe you arrange a weekly session for clients of both centers to participate in sensory art, meal preparation or music appreciation at either your location or theirs. Note that you have then created a superb opportunity for a news story.

Community involvement

Another smart way of gaining local visibility is through community involvement. Select an appropriate event and donate your space, time or money. Get parents and staff involved in the beginning. Then develop a marketing strategy for getting the word out about what you are doing. Consider using as many of these as possible to promote your center's involvement: posters, signs, flyers, press releases, staff, web site, reader boards, email and direct mail.

A few community involvement ideas: co-sponsor an event (such as a carnival for families or a series of parent education classes), donate your space for babysitting or CPR classes, install a community resource bulletin board, provide childcare for conference attendees at the nearby convention center or hotel, or sponsor a youth sports team.

Advertising

Advertising can be one of the most expensive methods of marketing, because you are paying for your ad to be seen by a lot of people. The problem is that it is difficult to directly target your potential customers. Although it is becoming increasingly easier to identify and target specific demographics such as geographic area, age and sex, it still is not cost-effective for small businesses with a relatively small number of customers. Think about the types of products and services you see advertised on television and in magazines: beverages, food, personal care items, cleaning supplies, automobiles, prescription drugs, movies and other television programs. Companies spend billions of dollars every year on advertising to the American consumer because a majority of us have a need for these products and base some of our purchasing on the commercials. You rarely see services, rather than products, advertised in mainstream media. They choose other methods to advertise. For corporate childcare companies, with over 20 centers serving thousands of children, television, radio or billboard advertising may be extremely beneficial when well placed, designed and negotiated. For the family childcare program serving less than 15 kids, you should concentrate efforts elsewhere.

If you are convinced that advertising is a good choice for you, research some of the less traditional forms such as: movie theaters, grocery carts and company newsletters, as those have the potential of reaching your target audience. Ask the advertiser for demographics of their audience and make sure they are also the audience you want to get in front of.

Canvassing

Canvassing is a bit like advertising in that the audience you are reaching does not necessarily need or want your services. The difference is that you spend a lot of time and energy to canvass and you spend a lot of money to advertise. If you are a small center or family childcare program, a flyer or promotional piece hand-delivered to homes and businesses in your neighborhood with a sincere and gracious "thank you" at the end of your sales pitch may help to spread the word of your existence, especially in close communities. If you plan on using this method, building relationships with the locations that are willing to help you is essential and usually a two-way street.

Flyers on bulletin boards, the windshields of cars or on doors are other canvassing methods. Canvassing is a very hands-on approach to marketing and often makes small business owners feel like they are at least doing something. Generally speaking, if not done politely and without permission, canvassing runs the risk of being irritating, even if effective.

Direct mail

You know what this is: those postcards you get in the mailbox from your dentist reminding you it's time for your next checkup or the brochure from your local community college. If used frequently and consistently, it can be an extremely effective method for keeping your name in the minds of your current families and potential ones.

You can purchase a mailing list and send your brochure to every address within your zip code that has a child under five years old in the household. Or you can send cards to your current customers thanking them for their business, promoting an event, sharing an article or any other reason you can think of.

Direct mail must be consistent to see results. If you cannot commit to sending a piece of mail to your mailing list at least once every two to three months, you should not rely on it as a main method of marketing. You can find a lot of detailed information on direct mail both in books and on the Web. These resources offer additional guidelines and tips to make your pieces more effective, such as: Spell every name correctly, use a first name if possible, use a stamp instead of preprinted bulk mail indicia, give them something to do with a deadline, and make the message of interest to the reader or give them a reason to save the postcard or brochure. Put a sticker on it with, "10% discount on first month's tuition when you bring this flyer in." Look at Appendix A under "Direct Mail" if you want to research further.

Signs

Signs (whether wooden, metal, glass, stone, etc.) can add a professional look and sense of longevity to your place of business, especially if you select one that can withstand years of abuse. Other times, you will find that you do not need a long-lasting sign. For these instances, you should look at inexpensive paper or vinyl banners or corrugated plastic. You might want to consider the increasingly popular auto magnets, large removable magnets that you can stick on your car when it is being used for business.

Sign shops are in nearly every community around the nation. Most of them offer reasonable rates and a plethora of materials, colors, typefaces and design skill. If you are in need of a sign, stop by the nearest sign shop and ask to see samples of their work. Then decide what you want on your sign. You can design it yourself (check with the shop for specifications), hire a professional designer or take your idea to the sign shop and let them do the design work for you.

Use your faculty

The teachers and other faculty members at your center (including yourself) are one of the many reasons parents selected your program. By giving staff what they need to represent the center, you are not only raising their personal level of professionalism, but also promoting your center using qualified representatives. Finding and retaining excellent teachers should be one of your main strategies for running a successful business. Potential customers may need to see your sign, brochure or web site to find you, but current customers see you every day. Use that to your advantage and prove to them that the decision they made to enroll their child in your school was the best decision they ever made. If you do, they will be the first to tell a friend or coworker about you and your team of teachers.

Consider the following when planning to use your faculty in your marketing strategy:

- Give everyone business cards. Each one is a mini-marketing piece. They help give your faculty members a sense of belonging and they offer a professional image for both your center and the individual.

- Make a plan to provide your faculty with industry training. Either hire a trainer to present workshops at monthly faculty meetings or take everyone to local and state conferences. Share what you learned with parents at an open house and/or post the successful completion of workshops on your bulletin board or web site.

- Train faculty members how to greet parents politely, even if they are in the middle of an activity with the children.

- Start a faculty-only referral program and offer incentives, such as paid time off, for helping increase enrollment.

Word-of-mouth

This is one of the most powerful forms of marketing available, and if you can harness the force of good word-of-mouth, you will have a waiting list a mile long. There is no single way to create it, but your goal should be to make potential customers familiar with your center to the point that they think of you when they think of childcare. This is what prompts word-of-mouth advertising, your most powerful and cost-effective method of gaining new enrollment. Remember that a bad reputation spreads about five times faster than good, so always do your best to maintain a positive reputation.

Welcome families

Connecting with the families you serve, beyond a smile and quick hello, is an excellent way to create a welcoming feeling at your program. Start by asking each family what you and your faculty can do to help connect their child's school experience with life at home. Consider developing a home visit schedule to talk with families in their environment. You will learn a lot about how you can better serve the child's needs while they are in your care by understanding what life is like at home.

A simple idea is to place photographs of your families on the wall at the children's eye level to help make the young ones feel more at home. Take that idea a step further and ask families to bring in something that represents their family or culture. You will have endless things to share with students that introduce them to the diversity both within the classroom and throughout the world. To create and develop a bond between school and home for the child, remember to use all items brought from home meaningfully. If you are uncertain what an item means for each family, ask them how to use it and how to show or explain its purpose to others.

A more obvious method of welcoming people is to put the word "welcome" on your sign, brochure and door in all of the languages you serve, or would like to serve. This is an indicator that, as a center, your doors are open to everyone. You can also choose to place the recognizable rainbow sticker in your window or on your brochure to welcome gay and lesbian families who are sometimes overlooked when cultural diversity in the classroom is encouraged or discussed. Ask families to share information about their life at home, but show respect by not pressuring them if you sense discomfort.

Making families feel welcome and at home in your center is another cost-effective method of creating positive word-of-mouth by establishing a high-quality program that serves everyone.

Chapter Three

That's Not What I Meant!

You only get one chance to make a first impression, so you need to know — and fully understand — what you want that impression to be. Ask yourself, "What are the most important things you want people to know and feel about your center?" Every type of marketing sends a message in the form of text, spoken words, design and delivery. If you are not careful, sometimes the message you are sending may not be the one you intended to send.

Take a look at the outdoor sign on the following page, for example. What message does it send to you?

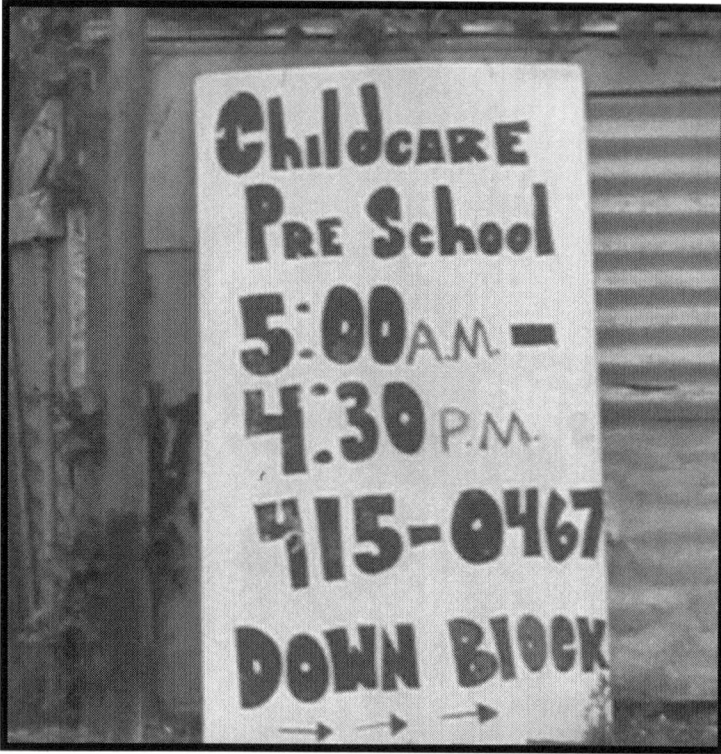

I drove by this sign every day for many months. Not long after I noticed it, I decided to take a photo and use it in my workshops to illustrate my point about unintended messages. Knowing what I do about the childcare industry and marketing, I assumed that the owner of this sign provides quality care in a nurturing environment, but that he/she did not understand what type of message was being sent.

Unfortunately, not everyone takes the time to investigate intended message. Some people might see this sign as unprofessional or sloppy, if all they are looking at is the sign. The problem the program encounters is

Making the commitment is worth it

As a trainer and on-site consultant, she was beginning to find herself in too many situations in which a business card would have helped market the services she provides. After serious thought and the assistance of a marketing professional, she decided to create a plan. The plan included several parts: goal setting, identity creation (or branding), design and copywriting, communications plan and a budget. The initial budget was only $1000.00, but it was used in the most cost-effective ways possible and without sacrificing quality.

Since the majority of her work involved direct interaction with people, the first step became the development of a logo, business papers and a brochure – items that she could carry with her and hand to people she met. A personal sense of accountability set in when she first sat in her office surrounded by boxes of marketing materials. Although she feared a lack of response, her determination to grow her business catapulted her into action. Within hours, she was implementing her plan: hand the client/prospect a brochure, engage in discussion about the eye-catching photo, end the conversation by exchanging business cards and then follow up with a letter in three days. This process dramatically changed the perception her clients, prospects and colleagues had of her and her company. The commitment she made was already getting people to take notice. Within a few months, she had generated so much activity that she was soon able to begin working on her newsletter and web site, both of which produced a company that now serves a national audience.

A newsletter full of relevant articles and helpful tips for anyone working with children is now expected in mailboxes every quarter and then posted in centers and programs around the country. (She often sees them on bulletin boards during site visits.) The web site attracts more and more clients every month and has proven to be one of the most reliable marketing tools she uses.

Marketing requires an enormous commitment, so completion of each step of the plan adds another layer of security for her clients. Based on her commitment to her organization and her clients, they know they have made the right decision to hire her. She confesses that her lack of patience and reluctance to loosen the purse strings are her biggest faults, but knows that her efforts and clients are worth every dime. She also acknowledges that, "consistency and excellent customer service have brought her trust, respect and success."

that the sign represents something else and people are forming a perception of what type of childcare is offered down the block.

Now, look at the sign in the photo below. What message does it send?

Approximately 12-18 months after I saw the first sign, this one went up. The drastic difference was not only eye-catching, but also intriguing. So much so that I waited another six months to learn how the new sign affected business for Friends Daycare. What I found out was that sales activity increased to a point where the owner had to have multiple signs made to communicate whether or not there were openings available at the

current time. Now when I drive by I see the "PROGRAM FULL: WAITING LIST" sign used for the cover of this book.

Are you sending any unintended messages?

Audience

Is the Wall Street Journal® written in the style of a children's book? Is a romance novel written like a non-fiction book? Why do you suppose neither is true? Because writers think about their audience–who is going to read a storybook to four-year-olds if it contains words like "transgression", "fastidious" and "rebuke?" The same is true for marketing. If a brochure looks and sounds like it is meant to engage a child, rather than the parents of that child, who is going to read it? The audience is important when writing, but you must also consider who your audience is when designing your brochure or web site.

Always keep your audience in mind. In other words, to whom are you talking? Who is your target audience and how best can you reach them? What types of materials do they expect from you and in what format do they expect information to be delivered? Flyers? Email? Newsletters? Hand-written notes? Daily conversation? Do they live in your zip code or do they work nearby? Are you marketing to highly professional people who expect updated information on your web site? Do you have a mixture of target audiences? If so, are you trying to increase any particular population? These are impor-tant questions to ask yourself when determining what sorts of materials and promotions are going to attract your target audience.

You are in an industry that walks a fine line between using a child-like approach or a less playful and more professional image. Although you care for, educate and nurture young children you must appeal to the families who make decisions about childcare placement. Balancing warm and nurturing essences with a clear, concise and professional message can be a complicated task. If you find yourself questioning whether or not a phrase, typeface, image or delivery method is appropriate, ask yourself this: "What are the expectations of my audience?"

Who are you?

Knowing how you want your business to be perceived before you begin creating signs or deciding which community events to sponsor is extremely important, and writing it down can help you get started on a path to understanding your business. Once you have written down what services you provide and how you want to be known, it is much easier to develop all of the tools you need to market yourself effectively. It means that you do not have to reinvent your message every time you want to run a promotion, add a page to your web site or develop a referral program.

ACTIVITY D-1

Your individual message should be a brief statement of seven to ten words about who you are, what you do and why you are the right choice for families. Coming up with seven words to describe your business is challenging, so let's start by writing a few paragraphs. Take out a several sheets of paper and write about the character of your business: location, services, staff, children, vision, etc. To help you begin, think about the answers to the following questions:

If someone else described your program or center, what would they say?

How is your center different from others?

What type of services do you provide that are unique or rare?

What is your vision for how you want your center to be perceived by others?

Is your faculty unique? Do you provide training for them? Do any of them have relevant degrees?

What are the benefits to a family if they select your program?

What is the most important thing you want people to know about your business?

ACTIVITY D-2

The previous exercise is meant to get you thinking about your vision, how you serve your customers, and what makes you different. The next step is to minimize the overall message by eliminating extraneous details. On a separate piece of paper, try to summarize what you just wrote into less than six sentences.

ACTIVITY D-3

To get to your final concise message of seven words, you need to narrow down the previous set of sentences one more time. Take the information from D-2 and cut it down to express your main message in less than ten words. This is who you are in a nutshell. It is not easy. Good luck!

The purpose of activities D1 – D3 is not only to develop a clear and concise message (D3), but to also provide you with text (copy) for your marketing materials. With a bit of editing to D1 and D2, you now have basic content for a brochure, web site, sign, flyer and other materials.

Writing, Editing and Proofing

Whether it's your web site, brochure, or a thank you note, a well-written, well-edited piece is fundamental to exhibiting your level of professionalism. Grab a dictionary, a thesaurus and a grammar guide for support during the writing process. (See Appendix A for recommended resources.) Remember your audience and make sure that you are writing for them.

Ask someone you trust to give you honest feedback on word choice and clarity of thought. Once you are ready to use your text, proofread it. Ask a minimum of three people (outside of the industry, if possible) who have never read it before to proofread it for spelling, grammatical, punctuation and typographic errors. Advise them to read through it several times focusing on one sentence at a time. Additionally, you can proof the text by reading it backwards, word for word. This sounds like a lot of work, but you will regret not doing it the first time your brochure comes back from the printer with the name of your center spelled wrong or your fax number where your phone number should be. Imagine the unintentional message you will send when your flyer reads, "Our teachers are qualified and well eduated." instead of "Our teachers are qualified and well *educated*."

Once you have edited your written message and placed it in your brochure, it is important to use it unchanged on all of your materials. Consistent use of your message helps build trust between your business and those to whom you are marketing.

Differentiators

What do you do that is different from other programs? What is it that your families appreciate about you or your staff more than anything else? Understanding what differentiates your program from the one down the street will help you in the creation of your marketing materials.

Most families in the United States need child-care, and some of them need it during nontraditional hours. It is difficult for parents to find quality programs that also meet their unusual circumstances, such as non-native English speakers or children with disabilities, so the better you can meet the needs of your clients, the more they will rave about you to their friends and co-workers.

ACTIVITY E

Most parents want to know how you can help reduce their stress. In other words, how you can save them time, money AND provide high-quality care for their children. Another method of developing a written message for your center is to determine what families want and then tell them how you provide the things they want in a way no other center can. This is one area in which your competitive research (See Chapter 2) helps you to create your own message.

Set up a matrix similar to the one on the next page and use it to determine your differentiators.

Service	Differentiator	Benefit	Communication
What services do you provide?	How is this service different from other providers?	How does this difference offer a benefit to parents and families?	How do you say this so people will pay attention and see value?
Hot Lunches	Our hot lunches are prepared by a certified nutritionist. Others do not use one.	Parent saves time (they do not have to prepare lunches) and is confident their child is eating healthy food.	Leave your worries about lunch and nutrition with us! Our chef is a certified nutritionist and creates fabulous hot lunches daily.

This exercise assists you in finding the key message for each of your services. Remember that you only need a few of these, but the better you get at determining and communicating how you can fill a need, the more people will pay attention to what you have to say.

Chapter Four

Smiles, Jammies and Mouthwash

Imagine walking into your local coffee shop to find the owner still in her pajamas, hair uncombed and sitting in a lounge chair reading the paper. After a minute or two, when she sees that you are standing at the counter waiting to order, she slowly gets up and walks to the register. Sighing heavily and admiring the polish on her fingernails, she asks, "What do you want?" You recoil as you begin to place your order because the sigh sent her morning breath sailing directly to your olfactory tubes. What would you do?

Now, imagine a father bringing his three-year-old to your childcare center. As he drives up, a staff member's car is parked in the space closest to the building and the garbage is overflowing out of the dumpster. When he walks into his daughter's classroom he finds yesterday's remnants of afternoon snack still on the counter and clothes all over the floor in dramatic play. The teachers do not greet him or the child because they are sitting in beanbags, drinking their coffee and talking about another staff member. What would he do? What should he do?

Before reading on, ask yourself and answer the following questions:

Do you view yourself as a professional?

Are you treated like a professional?

Do you act like a professional?

Do you treat your faculty like professionals?

Do they view themselves as professionals?

Do they act like professionals?

Merriam-Webster defines <u>profession</u> as:

> 4 a: a calling requiring specialized knowledge and often long and intensive academic preparation b: a principal calling, vocation, or employment c: the whole body of persons engaged in a calling

and a <u>professional</u> as:

> 1 a: of, relating to, or characteristic of a profession b: engaged in one of the learned professions c(1): characterized by or conforming to the technical or ethical standards of a profession (2): exhibiting a courteous, conscientious, and generally business-like manner in the workplace

---

The first step in becoming a professional is believing that you are one. Childcare professionals have usually obtained (and continue to acquire) specialized training to provide the children in their program with quality education and care based on specialized knowledge — similar to the requirements and development of other professions. Just because the training and education you receive may not come directly from highly prestigious and traditional academic settings does not mean it isn't valuable. You are providing care for the world's most precious asset and you must believe that your work is valuable.

The second step is to act like a professional. This chapter offers tips for examining your own level of professionalism, as well as ideas for introducing the subject to your staff. Acting like a professional does not necessarily mean putting on a suit and leaving your sense of humor at home. It simply involves becoming aware of how you or your center is perceived and then adjusting things you think may improve perception, thus increasing the number of phone calls, drop-ins and referrals.

Like other marketing methods, it takes a while for people to take notice and start talking about you and your program. (Remember to have patience.) Consistent professional behavior will only enhance your organization, helping to draw people in, but it is also what makes them stay and tell their friends about you. Imagine fifty or a hundred happy parents talking to friends, neighbors and family about the impression you and your staff make on them every day!

This particular area of business is not often considered marketing. Some view it as customer service or human resources, but small business owners understand that paying attention to the program's reputation is a smart way to run their business. Based on the way we defined marketing in Chapter 1, everything you do affects the perception others have of your center. That means you need to at least be aware of the subject and take necessary action to address any areas that you think will improve the way your center is perceived.

Excellent customer service is one of the best ways to differentiate your center and get noticed. Nordstrom® is known for their superior customer service and maintains a loyal customer base due to that commitment to service. I am one of those customers.

For my 12th birthday, my mom took me to the city for lunch. We stopped at Nordstrom where she bought me a new outfit as a gift. After wandering in and out of other stores, I suddenly realized that I didn't have the shopping bag with my birthday gift anymore. A retracing of our steps led us back to the sales counter at Nordstrom and as my mother asked the cashier if we had left the bag there, I noticed the clothing we had purchased spread on the counter behind the sales associate. She told us that a man had just returned the items and received cash in exchange. Then, without another word, the employee wrapped the shorts, shirt and earrings in tissue, placed them all in a new bag, walked the bag around the counter and handed it to me with a smile. You can't beat that type of service.

Of the items listed in Activity A, the following are often associated with professionalism and therefore need to be considered when assessing your center's level of professionalism: body language, business cards, center cleanliness, center orderliness, curb appeal, customer service, dress code, networking, personal hygiene, staff knowledge, telephone etiquette, thank you cards and tone of voice. Let's look at a few of them in more detail.

ACTIVITY F

1) Make a list of the qualities that influence your selection of a restaurant.

2) Make a list of the qualities that influence a family's selection of a childcare program.

3) Circle the matching ones. How many of the qualities apply to a dentist's office, a clothing store, or a salon?

Try this exercise with various other services. You will probably uncover the basics which are woven throughout all industries: CLEAN, FRIENDLY, GOOD SERVICE, GOOD PRODUCT, APPRO-PRIATE DRESS, ORGANIZED, PRICE, KNOWLEDGEABLE.

There are, of course, different expectations in different industries. For example, the owner of a small construction company is not always expected to wear a suit and tie or to be without a spec of dirt on him or her. There are occasions when his/her appearance is not what someone else might define as professional. However, a brief explanation from the construction company owner that he or she has been on a job site all day is usually enough to satisfy most discerning perceptions.

Verbal and written communication

How you say something is as important as what you say. Do you know anyone who has difficulty writing a simple thank you note or a summary of a child's day? Are they more effective communicating verbally?

Do you know anyone who has the opposite skill? They can communicate their message more thoughtfully if they write it down? This type of person may create a script for themselves when placing an important phone call or write out key points to cover during an upcoming conversation. There are both types in the world and you should try to identify which one you are and then use your strength to further the professional goals of your center.

If you are better at writing, make a habit of using that skill. Send home daily or weekly reports on how a child is doing, start a newsletter, or use email more frequently.

Email is another form of written communication that has become an integral part of business communication. From checking the status of an order to advertising a promotion, anyone doing business today is using email. However, as easy as it is to use, it's just as easy to misuse. In the fast-paced world we live in, typing an email and pressing send without considering the message you are sending happens too often. Think carefully about what you learned in Chapter 3 and how it is possible to send unintended messages. Are you thoughtful when composing your sentences and paragraphs? Is your message easy to understand? The use of email in business requires thoughtful sentences with correctly spelled words to maintain an adequate level of professionalism. Unfortunately, a confusing one with poor grammar, spelling, and punctuation is often more noticeable. Before pressing the send button, read your email through slowly and confirm that you have written a clear and concise message.

Although written communication is valuable and often unavoidable, some people are more comfortable with verbal communication. If daily reports are mandatory, but you do not feel comfortable writing them or think you cannot write a clear explanation of events, talk with the parents about what you wrote. Give them the in-depth explanation that you had difficulty writing. Be aware of non-verbal cues as you explore your verbal capabilities. Sometimes, tone of voice, eye contact, and body language send another unintended message.

Also consider how the parent(s) communicate best. Unfortunately, you are not always going to communicate in strictly one method, so you must also make an effort to improve your less effective method of communicating. Try watching others who have a natural talent for speaking with families and learn from them. Or, write a draft of a thank you note and edit it before committing it to the actual card.

Non-verbal communication

Non-verbal communication (or body language) expresses our feelings, emotions and thoughts without our mouths uttering a word. Due to various behaviors, your body may be sending an unintentional message. By understanding what is often conveyed by common body language, you can better identify and fine-tune your non-verbal communication skills. Body language is perhaps best at expressing emotions, and either supports or contradicts verbal communication. Understanding this is important because problems crop up when our body language is expressing something different than our words.

You may be telling a parent about the wonderful day you had with their child, but during your explanation you touched your cheek twice, did not smile, avoided eye contact, and had your arms crossed. When your body language challenges your words, the non-verbal cues are often believed over your verbal message, even if the parent does not realize it during the conversation. Evaluate the use of your own body language. Pay attention to what your body does as you talk to people, and take steps to adjust your non-verbal cues if you find that they regularly contradict what you are trying to say. It may seem strange at first, but after some practice smiling as you answer the telephone or greeting every person who walks into your classroom you will begin to feel more comfortable. Your self-assurance will shine through to the parents you greet, or at your next interview, or during the toast you have to make at a best friend's wedding.

A single message typically consists of more than one non-verbal cue. One of those cues is smiling. It is not always easy, nor does it always feel right, but you will be amazed at how a little practice is all it takes to perfect the skill and begin to feel an authentic smile. A smile helps makes the other person feel comfortable and secure. Flight attendants, receptionists and customer service personnel are all trained to smile. All staff should be trained to greet everyone who walks into your center with a smile. Smiles help reassure parents that they have made the right decision to leave their children in your care.

Eye contact is another dominant method of communication and can be viewed as communicating superiority or lack of respect by holding a gaze too intently. Or, if eye contact is not made, you communicate submission or lack of interest. To create a greater positive reaction from those you come into contact with, try a direct open gaze combined with a relaxed mouth.

Facial expressions and head movements are other

forms of non-verbal communication. The face is often the first part of a person we look at and basic emotions or thoughts are immediately focused on. A smile with teeth showing, open eyes and the head cocked slightly to the side indicates happiness. A fixed gaze, flushed skin, a sneer and the chin pointed downward shows anger. For more information on effective use of facial expressions, find a book on body language that includes a chapter or two on facial expressions.

Gestures complement other non-verbal forms of communication by offering a lot of expressiveness that is not always shown with facial expressions or eye contact. A few examples are shaking the fist in anger, raising your hand for attention or clapping in approval. Gestures can be used to communicate without words and are useful in noisy situations or when a language barrier exists.

The way you hold yourself can also express emotion. If you see someone hunched over with their head hanging down, you might assume that they are unhappy, depressed or submissive. On the other hand, a dominant personality or someone with confidence or hope tends to hold their shoulders back and keep their chin parallel to the ground or higher. Posture may also give you insight into a person's body image. Be aware of whether you slouch or project your chest out. You may be sending a message through posture that contradicts what you are saying. Western culture typically assigns the attribute of confidence to someone with a straight spine, shoulders back, a slightly lifted chin and a smile.

Also important to consider are distance and orientation. People differ in their comfort level in distance, depending on individual acceptance and culture.

Commonly accepted distances in the U.S. are generally six feet in public situations, three feet in social environments, and one foot or less in intimate conversation. In the childcare setting, you may find yourself unable to directly face the person you are talking to because you must keep an eye on the children. In these cases, a direct face-to-face orientation is difficult to obtain. The more direct the orientation, the more attention will be paid to the conversation.

Pay attention to how the person you are talking to responds to your body language and try to adjust if you see they are uncomfortable. It's generally appropriate to shake hands or offer a friendly pat on the back/shoulder in most business and social occasions. However, differences in culture often present themselves when communicating non-verbally and can result in some very interesting situations. Be aware that you are going to encounter a multitude of cultures and should be respectful of the individual's comfort level. For example, direct eye contact and close proximity is threatening or improper in many cultures, yet welcome and expected in others. Understand this when working with staff and the families you serve.

Telephone etiquette

Anyone who answers the telephone at work is one of the most important people at the company. They represent who that organization is and what type of service the person calling can expect. They are a reflection of the entire organization and thus have a lot of responsibility. A person selected for this duty should be trustworthy, organized and have a positive attitude.

Who do you rely on to answer the phone, offer information and take messages? Anyone answering the phone must be properly trained and prepared to answer questions. If you've given yourself that responsibility, have you taken the time to train yourself for this responsibility?

Did you know that smiling while talking makes you sound happier? Try saying hello with your mouth in a frown, a neutral position and in a smile. Which one sounds like a happy person ready to answer questions regarding childcare at your center? That's right, the smiling face. Train everyone to answer the business phone with a smile and your standard greeting. (see Activity G)

Write down the caller's name for reference later in the conversation. Listen carefully to what the other person is saying and answer their questions clearly and concisely. Ask them specific questions to help guide the conversation. Speak politely using terms such as thank you, you're welcome, good afternoon, etc.

Always follow up. If you took a message for someone make sure that they get it in written form. If there was an issue or question left hanging, you need to follow up by clearly communicating to the appropriate person who the caller was, what they wanted, when they needed it, and where to reach them. When you answer the telephone, you automatically take on the responsibility of making sure that the person you talked to is taken care of. This is part of practicing good customer service as well as exercising a component of professionalism.

Cellular phone use is so common that you can expect many of your callers to be on one. Remember to speak clearly and in short phrases, as coverage is not always perfect. I cannot tell you how many times I have been communicating extensive information only to realize that the call had been dropped.

ACTIVITY G

If you do not already have one, write a standard greeting for everyone who answers the telephone at your program. Type it up, print several copies and place one near every phone in the center. Then, practice answering the telephone using that greeting, but with different expressions and attitudes: a sad frown, an angry face, a bored attitude and a smile. Do you notice a difference in how you sound?

You will probably find that when you answer the telephone with a smile on your face, the tone of your voice is pleasant, establishing the basis for a positive encounter for the person calling. Practice always answering the phone with a smile. If you find yourself rushing to the telephone in an angry mood, consider letting the caller enter into voicemail or pause for a ring while you compose yourself. Remember: Telephone etiquette is often the first chance you get to make a good impression.

Dress and grooming

Dress and grooming are very personal and often sensitive issues to discuss. People are influenced by appearance, and cultural background often plays a part in their perceptions. This is important because it shows that we have some control over how others perceive us. Being aware of the impressions you make on others can help you communicate and interact with people. By simply adjusting our clothing choices and grooming habits, we can direct the perception of others. For example, the clothing that defendants wear to court is specially selected to persuade the jury or judge not to think of the defendant as a criminal, but as a person just like you.

Very few of us climb out of bed, dress in what we wore yesterday, and set out to confront whatever the day has to offer. We know that how we look and smell influences the way we feel about ourselves and how others react and respond to us. Appearance should be taken seriously if we want to further the mastery of professional behavior.

What are your daily grooming habits? Do you shower first thing in the morning? Do you apply makeup? Do you brush your teeth? Use mouthwash? Consciously select your clothing or put on the clothes you left on the floor? These are a few of the most common grooming habits among westerners. If you are an owner or director, consider supplying your faculty bathroom with mouthwash, toothpaste and other toiletries that staff can use to complement their own habits and meet their needs. As an individual, keep a small bag of toiletries (toothbrush, toothpaste, mouthwash, deodorant, hair brush, clear fingernail polish, etc.) at work or in your car for a quick touch up when you need it.

Style communicates a bit of who we are and how we view ourselves. If you have a dress code or are thinking about developing one, make sure that your reasoning is justified and try to keep personal preference out of the decision-making process. Consider first, what type of clothing is appropriate for working with children?

Childcare Professionals are:

Teachers, Directors, Trainers, Lobbyists, Business Owners, Children's Librarians, Administrators, Non-profit Staff Members, Psychologists, Professors, Researchers, Writers, Licensors, Politicians, Doctors, and so much more!

ACTIVITY H

Take a wardrobe inventory. Look through your closet and drawers to determine items that you can wear to work. What clothes do you have that are appropriate for work? What do you have that is not appropriate? Do you need to invest in anything new? Classify your items as:

    Should wear to work

    Can wear to work

    Should not wear to work

    Add to wardrobe for professional development

This activity is not meant to force you into changing your personal style, but simply to draw attention to the potential message you are sending to others about your level of professionalism. If you have an established dress code at your program, this is an activity you can use with staff to help them recognize the importance you place on appropriate dress at your center.

Keeping ourselves properly clothed can start to cost money that might be better used to buy food or airline tickets, right? If you have a faculty of more than two teachers, consider hosting an internal clothing drive. Ask all staff members to bring in items that do not fit or they have grown tired of (all must be in good condition and meet the dress code standards) so that everyone can benefit from a much larger closet. Make it a fun evening with an uplifting atmosphere by having a fashion show with a runway and announcer or have a party and require everyone to model an item they like or that they brought. If the first one is successful, make it an annual event so that faculty members can start collecting from family and friends ahead of time.

Professional development

Professional development is the continuing acquisition of knowledge and skills to improve your career. It proves to others and yourself that you are committed to the industry and the children. There is a variety of career paths within this industry, giving you the chance to work directly with children, families, trainers, policy makers, researchers, business owners and others. All require training, expertise or a degree, but mostly they require the passion and heart necessary to work in an industry that rewards its people with more joy than dollars.

Here are a few ideas to help you on your path:

- Join a professional association, such as National Association for the Education of Young Children (NAEYC) or National Association for Family Child Care (NAFCC).
- If you know what area interests you (or even if you do not know), volunteer on a committee for your local or state AEYC.
- Attend one or two extra trainings or conferences this year.
- Obtain your Child Development Associate (CDA) credential.
- Obtain proper certification to become a trainer in your state and begin delivering trainings in your area of expertise.
- Be an example for your faculty.
- Obtain national accreditation for your program.
- Volunteer to assist your local lobbyist to advocate for the industry.

- Offer financial assistance to your faculty for training and conferences.
- Write an article for an industry publication.
- Find a networking group in your area that fits your needs. If you cannt find one, start one.
- Read industry journals and other relevant publications to stay informed on current issues and new research.
- Keep yourself updated on the latest public policy concerning the early learning community.

What to say to your faculty

Issues of clothing, grooming, body language and telephone etiquette touch sensitive nerves of most people, and depending on the current relationship you have with your staff, it may be necessary to approach the topic slowly and gently. Try the activities recommended in this chapter or find other ideas to introduce the topics in a fun and non-threatening way.

After assessing yourself and your center, focus on one thing you would like to change each month. Maybe you want to work on greeting parents, telephone etiquette, dress and gossip in the workplace. If you try and bring all of these up at once in your next faculty meeting, you risk overwhelming your staff and yourself. Take a long-term approach and develop a monthly strategy for improving each one.

As the months pass by, revisit previous efforts with activities and reviews. If it takes longer than a month to see results, don't get discouraged. Take an extra month and keep working on it. Be careful not to beat a subject into the ground. Nothing gets the brush-off faster than repeated attempts to get staff interested in the same subject using the same material over and over and over. Leave it for a while and move on to something else.

Personal style, whether it is individual or cultural, is important to many people, so do not try to change it. All they need to do is meet a minimum level of requirements, whatever you determine those to be. Tell your faculty exactly what you expect so there is no confusion. For example, asking staff to wear appropriate clothing to work is not enough. You must be specific. No pajamas (except on pajama day) means no nightgowns, no slippers AND no flannel or cotton pants. If you allow skirts, how short is too short for working on the floor with children? If you allow the midriff to show, how much is too much to bare? An effective way to approach the dress code topic with your faculty is by asking them to help you define what is appropriate at your center. If everyone agrees to support the decisions made by the group, you have an excellent start to an appropriately dressed faculty.

Additional reasoning to offer staff is that a higher level of professionalism is good for the entire center. Professional behavior helps retain families/customers, thus preserving their jobs. Reasoning that is valid, but not necessarily effective with some is to remind them of job security. Much of what you are asking of them is probably in their job description or is listed as "other duties as assigned." Practicing good parent relations is a form of marketing that keeps the center running, allowing staff wages to be paid.

Presenting the basics of professional behavior to your faculty benefits them in the long run. If they ever seek other employment, their chances of being hired are increased. Understanding their options regarding types of positions the industry has to offer gets them excited about their career choice and their job. Help them understand what their options are for exploring more education in the field of early learning.

These are real issues in childcare settings and should be addressed with care and the understanding that it will take weeks or months to change behavior. Lead by example and be patient. Find books on related topics and research the issues on the Web, join a networking group of directors and ask what they're doing, or hire someone to work with you or your staff.

ACTIVITY I

Ask your staff to research gestures among various cultures. What do common gestures in the US mean around the world? This approach helps introduce the subject of cultural variations in non-verbal communication. For example, the "thumbs up" gesture doesn't mean the same thing in Australia as it does here in the states. Emphasize the point that because there are so many variations of gesture meanings, that it is wise to refrain from using them.

ACTIVITY J

Play charades! Create three categories: EMOTIONS (angry, elated, etc.), PERSONALITY TRAITS (funny, shy, etc.), TV SHOWS. Separate into teams and begin to play. (Find official rules online.) The purpose of playing charades is to illustrate how the use of non-verbal communication can express a concept or point when other forms of communication cannot be used.

ACTIVITY K

Use "Activity G" as a basis for working with your faculty. Have them practice your standard greeting and show them where you have placed the printed versions.

Prepare a script of a typical phone call from someone looking for information on your program to help facilitate role-playing. Ask participants to find a partner and give one person the caller script. The other person gets to "answer" the telephone and the caller's questions. To help them feel more comfortable with the activity, offer them some guidance by acting out the call yourself before they get started.

You can also prepare other scripts to give your staff practice at handling telephone calls. Consider developing a script with an upset parent about a common complaint or one from a person who has so many questions, the conversation is taking the teacher away from the classroom for a long period of time. Remember that the activity is an opportunity to teach staff members how you want them to represent the program.

Not only do you sometimes have to struggle with other people's perceptions of what kind of center you run, but also there is a general lack of professionalism in many areas of everyday life. Whether this is because of the fast pace we are all living or some other reason, poor service and unfriendly encounters make professionalism a good method to employ. Best of all, it does not require any money to write a telephone script and train your teachers to smile when a parent walks in the room.

Professionalism is about respect and understanding. No matter which line of work a person is in, the common thread of professionalism centers around respecting yourself and others and understanding the expectations of the people you work with, including faculty members, vendors, families and prospects.

All of the details surrounding this topic can be overwhelming, and constantly worrying about how others perceive you can be counter-productive. If you are looking for a simple set of guidelines, here it is:

- Be generally respectful to everyone.
- When faced with a situation in which you are unsure of how to behave, follow the lead of the other person.
- Smile.
- Say please and thank you.
- Keep yourself and your clothing clean.
- Wear clothing appropriate for working with children and families.
- Do not gossip.

Not all of these areas of professional behavior are relevant to everyone or every program, nor is it expected that you and your faculty should interact and dress according to unrealistic expectations. Select the things you think are important to your business and analyze their effectiveness. If you find that there is room for adjustment or improvement, develop a plan for implementing those changes. Just be aware that how your business is perceived often has a direct effect on how (not if) your business succeeds.

Professionalism Assessment Questions

These questions are intended to start you thinking about your personal professionalism. Answer them honestly and if you find any problem areas, look closely at exactly what the problem might be. Then determine what you want to do about it (if anything). This list of questions can also be a useful activity when working with faculty members.

- *Are you better at verbal or written communication?*

- *Have you ever been told that after getting to know you, you are not at all what that person expected?*

- *Has anyone ever told you that they are intimidated or afraid of you?*

- *Do you think that people often do not understand what you have said to them?*

- *Do you find yourself uncertain of what to say when you answer the phone at work?*

- *Do you have trouble finding appropriate work clothing in your closet?*

- *Has anyone ever told you to stand up straight?*

- *Do you brush your teeth and wash your body before going to work every day?*

- *Do you respect authority?*

- *Are you respected?*

- *Do you always greet parents with a smile?*

- *Are you a member of a professional organization?*

- *Do you attend trainings and/or conferences specific to your work in childcare?*

- *Are you a member of a local networking group that shares ideas and knowledge about the profession?*

- *Are you interested in pursuing another job within the child-care industry? Do you know the process for getting there?*

Chapter Five

Design Basics

This chapter provides those of you who do not have time to take a design class or perform extensive research on typeface and color usage with guidelines for creating marketing pieces. There are so many fonts, colors, software programs and paper to choose from that it is easy to get carried away. Try not to. A good rule of thumb is: less is more. If you have too much text for the size of paper you are printing your brochure on, edit it.

Before starting to design any marketing piece you need to identify your audience, the purpose of the piece, how it will be used and its shelf life. For example, if you are hosting an open house and are creating a postcard to announce the event, you should identify the following:

Audience

Faculty, families and community

Purpose

Ask people to visit the school, meet the teachers, and meet the families of other students

Intended use

Mailed and hand-delivered, left at local businesses, sent home with parents, posted on bulletin boards

Shelf life

Six weeks

Next, let's look at some of the elements you might encounter when creating marketing pieces, such as brochures, signs, postcards, flyers and web sites.

Logo

A logo is a graphic representation of your business, and it should be a consistent design element on your web site, brochure, signs and other marketing materials. Whether it consists of type, a graphic mark or both, your logo identifies your childcare center to parents, staff and the public. With consistent use, it becomes an essential piece of your marketing design and strategy. If you do not already have one, you should hire a professional designer to create one for

Tip: To draw attention to areas of information, use color sparingly and thoughtfully, such as creating a single color background to only one area of text.

Caution: Too many colors and drastic changes in color can distract the reader from the content of your marketing piece.

you.

Once you have a logo, use it consistently. Take care not to stretch or rotate your logo when you're adding it to a brochure or your web site, and make sure the colors always look the same. It does not always require prominent placement, but your logo should be used on most of your marketing pieces.

Color

People create abstract, sensory, emotional and object associations to colors, so color can be used as a powerful method to communicate. The use of color in design can evoke particular emotions and associations. For example, red is often associated with danger (abstract), heat (sensory), passion (emotional), or tomato (object). These associations are often based on cultural background and life experience, so be aware of your audience and how the use of color may affect their response. Do some research and make the best possible selection. A common example of this is that the traditional color of mourning in many Asian cultures is white, yet white is used in western cultures to communicate purity, innocence, and cleanliness. Below are some examples of common associations with color.

Red: bravery, danger, spice, heat, apples, tomatoes, passion, anger, luck

Blue: trustworthy, confident, sky, protective, cold, water, peace, tranquility, sadness

Yellow: light, sun, happiness, optimism, hope, lemons

Green: ecological, freshness, growth, rebirth, grass, envy

Orange: citrus, bright, tasty, energy, pumpkin

Purple: nobility, grace, eggplant, depth

Brown: earth, comfort, chocolate, wood

Tip: If you need to save money by using only one ink color, consider using brown or dark blue instead of black. It softens the look and you can use various shades of the color to create the illusion of more color.

Caution: Large areas of light shading often print less rich than the darker shades. Using the shading as a background for text helps lessen this effect. If you lay type over a background, make sure the two colors contrast enough so that the reader can easily see the text.

Grey: stability, modern, cold, elephants, concrete

White: purity, peace, death, brightness

Black: modern, conservative, structure, mysterious, death

Printing

Small businesses have several options for printing, but we'll only address the three most common forms for small businesses.

Offset Lithography: This is a very common method for printing large quantities of brochures, postcards, etc. For large orders (over 5000), this might be your most economical choice. If you decide to use offset printing, plan ahead because turn-around time can take longer than other processes. Design, revision, proofing and file preparation are important steps in every project, and working directly with the printer helps guarantee a high-quality finished product.

Four colors of ink (Cyan, Magenta, Yellow, Black – CMYK) are mixed together to create a rich palette of colors. (You can see this palette by ordering a swatch book from Pantone® or by simply asking to view your printer's copy.) Using color adds interest and attracts people to your marketing piece, but it also adds cost for each color you use. One color is less expensive than two and two is less expensive than three or four, but you will find that there is little cost savings between three and four color printing. The use of color should be considered during the planning and design phase. Before you dismiss the possibility of color, talk to your printer for additional cost-saving ideas. If you can afford to print in color, do it.

Digital: This is the best way to get small quantities (1-1000) printed for an affordable price. Due to the fast pace of these printers, you can often get your print job back in days. The best part is that the cost does not go up as you add color. These printers can be found online and they accept several types of files and may even provide other services such as pre-designed templates and full design services. *See Appendix A for printing resources.*

At home: Home and small office printers are more advanced than ever before. If your budget limits your printing capabilities, try using your own first. Abide by the same design guidelines and see how it turns out. Choose a nice paper type, and keep the packaging in a file for future reference. To save even more on printing costs, check with your local library. Many offer free or low cost color or black and white prints and/or copies.

Layout

When deciding where to put your heading, logo, phone number, photo and other graphic elements, try to prioritize and form a hierarchy of importance for each one to help walk the reader through the information. You want to draw the reader from the top to the bottom and if it's a folded piece, you want them to open it. For example, your fees or rates are important, but do they belong on the front panel of your brochure? Probably not. Your center's name, logo or other graphic element

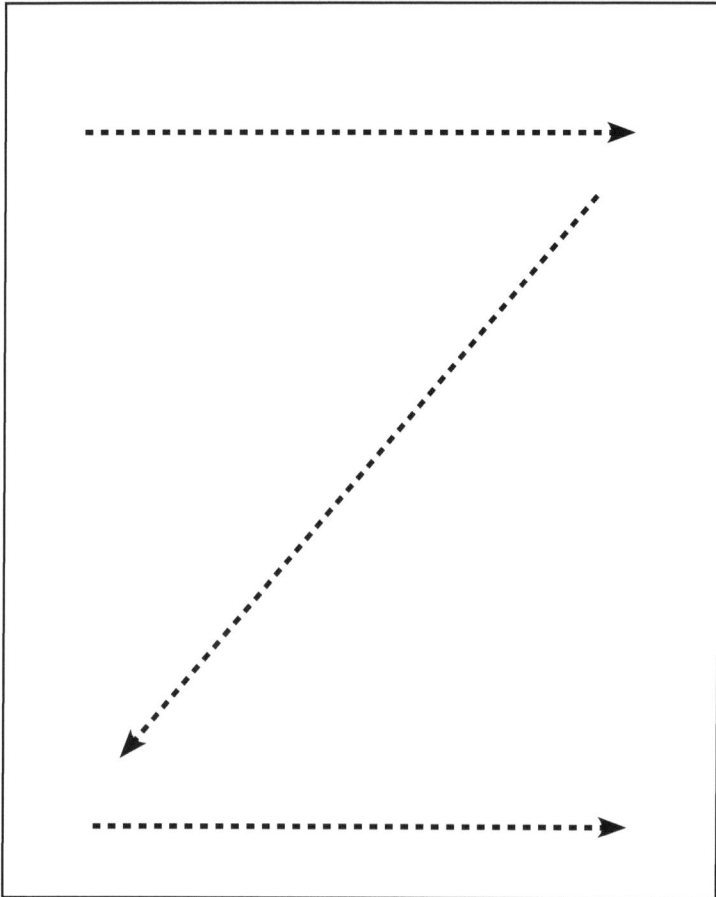

By prioritizing the information on your materials, you can often eliminate extraneous details and create a more open design that is easier to comprehend quickly.

that introduces your program is enough. You can also add a line or two of text that entices the reader to open your marketing piece.

People (in most western cultures) tend to scan direct mail, flyers, brochures and other materials. For this reason, you want to place your most important text in the scanning area. This takes the shape of a Z: top, left to right, down to the left, then back across to the right at the bottom. Other cultures read right to left and are thus influenced by habit. Then, a different layout may be essential to effective communication.

Empty space (aka: white space) is ok and an essential element in most communication designs. Do not fill every inch of space with words or images. Empty space is relaxing to the eyes and helps you control the importance of the content. See the business card examples in this chapter for a sample comparison of design with and without white space.

Using Text

Your text may be the most important message on the marketing piece, but if there are too many words or if it isn't organized, you risk losing your reader. Use typeface and design to guide the reader through the levels of importance using size, weight and color. Using larger bold text draws focus to headings, and subheadings help break up and organize large quantities of text. Space between lines of text is called leading or paragraph spacing. Space between letters and words is called kerning, tracking, or character spacing. Adjust these to add attention-grabbing elements to your headings, lists and blocks of text.

Try to keep the number of fonts used to two on a single piece, three at the most. For the sake of consistency, write down your final typeface selection and keep it near the computer for quick reference when you are typing a letter or designing your brochure.

Heading in Arial Black 14, centered

Subheading in Arial 10 bold, aligned left

Text is in Arial 10 and aligned to the left. Lorem ipsum dolor sit amet, consectetuer adipiscing elit, sed diam nonummy nibh euismod tincidunt ut laoreet dolore magna aliquam erat volutpat. Ut wisi enim ad minim veniam, quis nostrud exerci tation ullamcorper suscipit lobortis nisl ut aliquip ex ea commodo consequat.

Duis autem vel eum iriure dolor in hendrerit in vulputate velit esse molestie consequat, vel illum dolore eu feugiat nulla facilisis at vero eros et accumsan et iusto odio dignissim qui blandit praesent luptatum zzril delenit augue duis dolore te feugait nulla facilisi.

Subheading in Arial 10 bold, aligned left

Nam liber tempor cum soluta nobis eleifend option congue nihil imperdiet doming id quod mazim placerat facer possim assum.

Subheading in Arial 10 bold, aligned left

Nam liber tempor cum soluta nobis eleifend option congue nihil imperdiet doming id quod mazim placerat facer possim assum.

Line length

In general, columns of text are easier to read quickly. However, you must be careful not to make the column too narrow, as the text becomes difficult to comprehend.

It is usually easier for readers to quickly understand what you are trying to communicate if you use columns instead of long lines to express your message.

It is usually easier for readers to quickly understand what you are trying to commu- nicate if you use columns instead of long lines to express your message.	*It is usually easier for readers to quickly understand what you are trying to communicate if you use columns instead of long lines to express your message.*

**Which one of these is easiest
to quickly understand?**

Justification

Small amounts of text can be read in any alignment, but it is common for the majority of western readers to prefer left alignment of text and major headings centered.

```
XXXXXXXXXXXX
XXXXXXXX
XXXXX
XXXXXXXXXXXXXX
XXXXXXXXXXXXX
XXXXXXXXXXXX
XXXXXX
XXXXXXXXXXXX
```

left alignment

```
    XXXXXXXXXXXX
      XXXXXXXX
        XXXXX
   XXXXXXXXXXXXXX
   XXXXXXXXXXXXX
    XXXXXXXXXXXX
      XXXXXX
    XXXXXXXXXXXX
```

center alignment

```
        XXXXXXXXXXXX
          XXXXXXXX
            XXXXX
     XXXXXXXXXXXXXX
      XXXXXXXXXXXXX
       XXXXXXXXXXXX
           XXXXXX
       XXXXXXXXXXXX
```

right alignment

Using color in text

If you decide to design and print your materials in color, you should choose a dark color for your text more often than not. Black, dark brown, dark blue, and dark grey are your best choices. Dark purple, dark green and maroon are fine to use. Yellow, red, pink, lavender, light grey, light blue, and other light colors have trouble being seen by the reader. Remember that you are trying to communicate with a reader and if the words on your brochure, web site or poster are difficult to read, you risk losing potential customers because they do not have time to figure out what you are trying to tell them.

Tip: Adjust the line, paragraph, word and letter spacing to add a simple and clean look.

Caution: Try not to disturb the standard shape of words, as it causes problems for the reader.

Examples

There is less space between lines in this portion of text. Space between lines is called leading. Less space between lines in this portion of text. Space between lines is called leading. Less space between lines in this portion of text.

There is more space between lines in this portion of text. Space between lines is called leading. More space between lines in this portion of text. Space between lines is called leading. More space between lines in this portion of text.

Subhead with less letter and word spacing

Subhead with more letter and word spacing

Borders and bullets

Decorative elements, such as borders and bullets, should be used in moderation. Separating text inside a box to highlight a specific collection of information is effective, especially if used infrequently and consistently. Try organizing your text in ways that create visual separation without lines. The edges of

> *Tip: A border helps focus attention to text or images by framing the information.*
>
> *Caution: Too many of them confuses the reader and disrupts the flow of content.*

your columns of text can be used to produce a false impression of a border, as well as using enough white space between columns.

Bullet points of all shapes and sizes are helpful when trying to draw attention to a list. Make sure whichever bullet you select (circle, arrow, mailbox, etc.) complements the rest of your design. Eliminate the need for bullets by increasing the space between the lines or paragraphs of your list.

Images

Photographs and other graphic images add dimension to your message and enhance the design of your materials. Posters, large flyers, small postcards and the web all require different files for the same image. The larger the printed image, the more resolution you need.

Let's say you have a photo you want on your brochure and web site. The image on the brochure is 3"x5" and the web site image is even smaller. As long as your original digital image is more than 150 dpi (dots per inch) at 3"x5", the print quality should be adequate.

Just save another copy of the image as a .jpg or .gif and reduce the dpi to 72 for your web site or use the "save for web" option in Adobe Photoshop®. If you have a digital camera, set it to the highest resolution available. Your pictures will use more space, but you can always take away dpi (make the photo smaller), but you cannot add dpi to a photo to make it print better at a larger size.

> Tip: Consider cropping your image to reveal only a detail of the photo to create visual interest.
>
> Caution: Removing too much might remove the context of the original image.

Here are *general guidelines* for dpi when working with digital images:

Line art: 1200 dpi (saved as .bmp)

Poster: 600 dpi (saved as .tif or .eps)

Large print: 300 (saved as .tif or .eps)

Small print: 150 (saved as .tif or .eps)

Web: 72 dpi (saved as .jpg or .gif)

When using clip art, make sure you have the right to use it and are not infringing on copyright. Also, consult your overall message/brand strategy and decide if the use of clip art represents your program.

When using photographs of the children in your program, get the proper written permission. If you find yourself unable to snap the right photo, use stock photography. To view libraries of thousands of images, visit: istock.com, creatas.com, jupiterimages.com, getty-images.com, or veer.com.

Web site

A web site can be one of your most cost-effective methods of marketing. The number of potential visitors to your site is limitless, but you need to design it to meet the needs of your target audience.

If you have determined that your audience wants or needs you to have a web site, do not let a fear of technology or thoughts of high price keep you from setting one up.

Follow these steps to get started:

1) Secure your URL / Domain / Web address: www. yourcenter.com. You can do this through several companies. I use Verio at verio.com. The cost is around $10 for 1 year, $20 for 2 years and so on.

2) Determine who is going to host your site. You need a server to store your web pages. Sometimes your Internet service provider (ISP) has packages you can purchase. Or, you can find a company that specializes in hosting web sites, such as: Verio®, Speakeasy®, Volusion®, Yahoo®, or WorkZ Sites®. Some of them help you build your site with easy-to-use design templates. Unless you are planning to place a lot of images and graphics on your site or take credit cards, you won't need an expensive hosting package. Those under 10MB of web space should suffice.

3) Set up access to your web-hosting server (this information is usually included in emails from your hosting company).

4) Structure your site. How many pages do you need? Do you want to have room to grow? How

do you want to plan for that? You will probably find that just getting started requires more than a single page. Sometimes it helps to create a diagram of your site for a visual reference of how the pages will relate to one another and what type of content you need to write. (See the next section for tips on what you should start with.)

5) Begin the design and publication of your web site. As mentioned in step number two above, some of the web hosting companies help get you started by providing design template, or you can even pay them a little extra to design the site for you. Alternatively, you can hire a web designer, ask a parent if they can help or purchase one of several web publishing software programs to do it yourself. Those include: Microsoft® FrontPage®, Adobe GoLive®, Macromedia Dreamweaver® and others.

6) Test your web site to make sure all of your links work and images show up. Ask others to review it for grammar, punctuation and spelling.

7) Once you have your main structure and design finalized, remember the importance of consistency. Keep your basic content, structure and design unchanged. However, you should update the content as often as possible to keep people interested.

8) Use your site to communicate with families about what is happening at your center. Post events and update it monthly or weekly. Send emails with links to your web site and encourage everyone to check your site for the updated details.

9) As you get comfortable with making changes, think about adding pages that are relevant and helpful to parents. Offer links to hot topics in your center. If parents are concerned about a specific issue, create a page to help guide their own research on the topic. Make it a useful tool and not just a few static pages of information.

You have the option of setting up your web site with as many pages as will meet the needs of your customers. Since most users typically scan the page looking for keywords, a simple structure with small sections of content makes the site user-friendly by taking people through the site quickly and easily.

A single home page with basic contact information may suffice or you may need a complex set of pages consisting of the following pages: Home, About/ Philosophy, Services, Classes, Rates, Faculty, Contact, A Day in the Life of Your Preschooler, Newsletter, Newsletter sign up, Pay online, Photos and Events.

See the next page for a simple site diagram example.

Consistency

Just like message, once you have decided on your typeface, color palette and bullet style, it is extremely important to use them unchanged on all of your materials. Consistent use helps build confidence in your business.

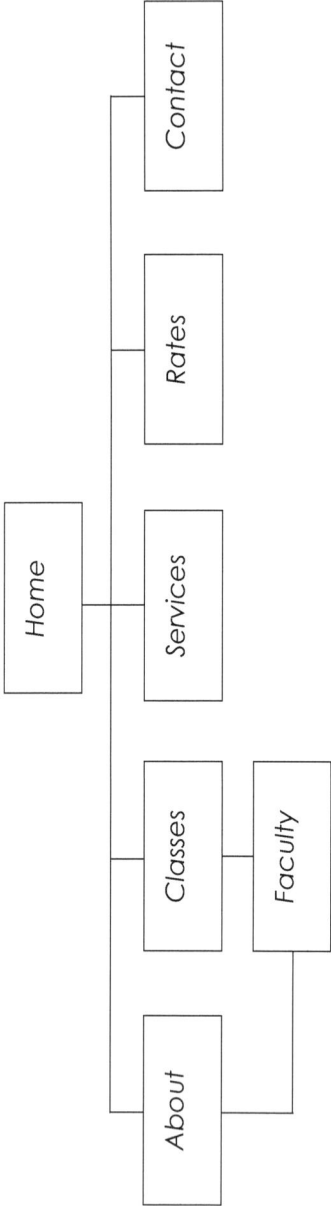

A simple site diagram helps you organize your information.

Quick reference design tips

- Try to keep the number of fonts used to two or three on a single piece.
- Check with your library for printing costs and limits.
- Ask a parent or two you trust to give feedback on your latest brochure before you print all of them.
- Use related typeface throughout all materials to strengthen an overall professional image.
- Use graphic elements to help guide your audience through the content.
- Digital printing is often your most cost-effective choice for small quantity color materials.
- Use a different color instead of black on a two-color design to create the effect of printing in several colors.
- Simplicity attracts the over-stressed parent.
- Use columns to separate text into readable blocks.
- Make sure that you get the proper written permission to use photographs of the children in your center.
- Your audience should not have to fight with graphics to see the content. Avoid complicated backgrounds and borders.
- The design is for your audience. Consider their needs, skills and cultural background.
- Avoid using anything in your design that does not support your overall message.

- Think about cultural backgrounds of your audience when designing. Many read right top to bottom left and others read top left to bottom right. This influences the way people look at your piece.
- Build your web site with small amounts of text on lots of pages to keep users actively moving through the information.

Double-check

Make sure you have the following on your marketing piece:

Center name

Phone number

Address (Some family childcare businesses do not list addresses for security purposes. If this is what you do, think about writing "Please call for address and directions.")

Web address (URL)

Cost info (If pricing changes regularly, this could be an insert for your brochure. Or, ask readers of the brochure to visit your web site for pricing details.)

Accreditation status

Date of event (NOTE: Putting a date on a marketing piece automatically determines its shelf-life.)

Chapter Six

Budget? What Budget?

Marketing costs money. There are very few methods that do not require at least some amount of money to implement. In order to take marketing and the growth of your business seriously, you must allocate funds for your annual marketing budget in the same way you plan for salaries, rent and electricity.

Some companies spend close to 30% of their gross sales on marketing. Depending on your goals and other budgeted items, 10-15% should be enough to get you started. For example, if you have monthly sales of $10,000.00, your marketing budget should be at or near $1,000.00 - 1,500.00 per month or $12,000.00 – 18,000.00 per year. Do not forget that this includes ALL of your marketing efforts: web site, faculty training, newsletter, telephone book listing, business cards, signage, etc.

Based on our definition of marketing in Chapter 1, you could potentially itemize all of your expenses in the marketing budget. However, for ease of creating a marketing budget, include anything that you have determined to be specifically related to increasing the sales activity at your program. Obvious examples are the creation of a new brochure or training for your faculty. Not-so-obvious examples are the cost of postage to mail the new brochure or the printing costs of the flyers to announce to families and the public the successful completion of training for the teachers.

Along with your marketing plan (which we will discuss in the following chapter), your budget should be put together annually. On the next page, I have included a basic budget for your reference.

Hire someone or do it yourself

Working with designers, writers and printers can be intimidating for many reasons. However, hiring someone to provide good design, quality printing, or clear writing can save you hours of frustration. Find a professional who has the expertise you need and offers guidance, but who ultimately respects your decisions as the client. For successful interactions with vendors, be explicit in your expectations, ask for consistent communication from the contractor and get the price quote in writing.

Doing your own marketing is less expensive, if you understand and practice the fundamentals of good

Sample Annual Budget

Advertising **$1,800**
        Yellow pages $1,100
        Community newspaper $700

Web site **$850**
        Hosting $300
        Design $550

Open House **$300**
        Food $150
        Flyers $75
        Decorations $75

Staff Training (10 hrs) **$1,150**
        Independent trainer fee $1000
        Announcements $150

Field Trip T-shirts **$550**
        Adult sizes $160
        Child sizes $390

New Brochures **$660**
        Designer fee $440
        Printing $220

Direct Mail Campaign **$1,670**
        Design (4 postcards) $800
        Printing $640
        Postage $230

Outdoor Sign Cleaning **$250**
        Service Fee $250

Paint Inside Classrooms **$400**
        Paint supplies $250
        Food for volunteers $150

Referral Program **$1,230**
        Printing $230
        Incentives $1,000

Business Cards for All Staff **$470**
        Design $240
        Printing $230

Total **$9,330**

design (see Chapter 5), message development (see Chapter 3) and are technologically savvy. You can create your own marketing pieces to save yourself money, and you may enjoy the creative process.

Although spending money is unavoidable, spending lots of it is not necessary. There are several books and articles on shoestring budgets that you should definitely read. (see Appendix A)

Here are a few tips and guidelines to help you save money:

- Assess your printing needs and select the appropriate method based on your budget and message. (see Chapters 4 & 5)

- Check, double-check and triple-check spelling and other details on your marketing pieces. You often do not get to proof before printing, unless you specifically request it.

- Free or inexpensive business card resources: vistaprint.com, dcp-print.com, overnightprints. com, printingforless.com.

- Check with your library. You may be able to print limited color or black and white pages for free.

- Ask for the most economical paper stock, but make certain it does not compromise your overall message.

- Proofread!!! Ask three or four different people to proof materials. Try to find people with various backgrounds and perspectives. Read it backwards word-by-word. Use plain paper to block all but one line. Check any questionable words letter by letter with a dictionary.

- Most printers use standard paper size for printing, so plan ahead by understanding that to keep costs down, your design must fit within 8 1/2" x 11" or 11" x 17". Bleeds (color to the edge of the final cut piece), folding and cutting all cost extra.

- Postage varies based on weight and size. A large postcard measuring 8 1/2" x 5 1/2" (half of a sheet of 8 1/2" x 11") costs the same as a letter to mail. Check the United States Postal Service web site (usps.gov) for current size restrictions for postcards, letters, and other pieces.

- Bulk mail can also save you money, because you do not pay your staff to apply labels and stamps. If you have a mailing list of over 500 names, you should look into this option. Ask your printer for the name of a reputable mail house.

- Plan ahead to avoid rush orders. Printers charge extra for these. Make sure you have plenty of time for this part of the process. Ask them what their turn-around time is for your job and allow two or three extra days for unexpected problems. If a mistake is made (especially if fault may lay with the printer), try to reason with them for a reduced price to reprint.

- Magazines and newspapers have their own designers for you to use in the event that you do not have a pre-designed advertisement. If possible, avoid using this service. Because they are getting paid by the publication, they have less of an interest in understanding your business, target audience and message. Spend the money on a designer to layout your first advertisement and then use that ad for the rest of the year. You may even be able to bundle the design work and get a postcard, brochure and ad for a lower price than you think.

- Find multiple uses for materials. Use your postcard or flyer at the open house, then use it again for your direct mail campaign, and again at a community event.

- Think ahead to possible changes in address or phone numbers. Print small quantities if you expect any alterations. Try to avoid using dates, except when promoting a specific event. You can use inserts for details that change regularly, such as cost or activities. How long do you need to be able to use it without making changes? A brochure can often live for two or three years without any major changes.

- If something does change, like the addition of a URL for your new web site, a simple sticker cut to size can be placed inconspicuously under the address. This can help prolong the shelf life of your piece.

- Join forces with another agency. If there is another business close by, ask if they want partner with you on a marketing piece: they get one half, you get the other. Or partner with another childcare center across town and sponsor an event. You will be pleased with what you can afford when you are splitting the costs.

- Practice excellent customer service. It is the least expensive and most effective means of marketing.

- Stick to your plan. Changing your marketing plan requires you to spend more on production and dilutes your overall effect.

- Create your own survey for research. Look for examples online to help you with how to word the questions. To get usable information, questions need to be clearly stated with little or no room for interpretation. Surveys should also be quick and easy to fill out. Otherwise, your response rate will be low.

- Market primarily to customers instead of prospects. Good word of mouth spreads fast and is a reliable method of marketing. When trying to keep costs low, focus on your current clients. Offer a referral program, parenting classes, industry research, etc.

- Market to your target market. If you have the opportunity to get directly in front of your target market through a community event, direct mail, etc., do it. Your cost-effectiveness increases if you can market directly to them. For example, an advertisement in the local paper is not usually as cost-effective as an advertisement in the parenting newsletter from your local college.

- Ask to borrow the labor of your families and hold a volunteer work party for a specific project. Or ask for one parent's expertise in whatever it is you are lacking: Web design, printer knowledge, contacting the media, etc. As long as you are a gracious recipient of the help and don't abuse your volunteers, you may find this to be a very valuable source of assistance.

Non-profits

If you are a non-profit, you can take advantage of benefits not available to other childcare operators. Aside from the tax benefits and reduced postage costs, you can ask for donations and discounts. Of course cash gives you more flexibility, but see if your office supply store will donate or discount paper, ink, labels or other marketing supplies. Ask printers for a discounted rate on printing your brochures, flyers and business cards. Ask software suppliers for donated software and grocery stores for food donations for your next event.Always thank donors with a thank you card (signed by the kids, if it is a large donation), a notice in your newsletter and/ or on your web site, and the proper tax receipt if you are a 501(c)(3).

Measuring your efforts

Marketing efforts overlap, so you must pay attention to which efforts are working and which are not. For example, if you have your phone number listed in the telephone book white pages (print and web), two resource and referral web site links, have a brochure, great location, well-placed sign and a web site – you have eight different efforts running at the same time (not to mention possible customer or staff referrals and word-of-mouth). How do you know which ones are working? More importantly, how do you know which ones are not? You could be spending a lot of money on a phone book listing that is not bringing you any business.

We will talk more about measurement in the next chapter. For now, just understand that by knowing which efforts are working and which ones are not, you can save yourself dollars and maybe even apply the savings to a more cost-effective method.

Chapter Seven

Bringing It All Together

Once you understand that marketing is more than your brochure, web site and yellow pages ad (although they can be crucial components of the overall marketing plan), you need to formulate your long- and short-term goals and put your plan in writing. A marketing plan helps you gather the details of your marketing activity in one document, and offers a framework for applying the knowledge of your program's strengths and obstacles into a workable plan. It also provides a concrete list of marketing efforts to be measured. By knowing which of your efforts are effective, your future decisions about planning for marketing are made easier.

Setting goals

Your long-term goals are the foundation for the success of your short-term marketing efforts and are enveloped in your overall plan. Formulating long-term goals, such as positive customer service or consistent use of message, is crucial to the positive long-lasting impression and overall perception that the short-term goals achieve.

Long-term goals include revising things such as: dress code, pricing, cleanliness, hours of operation, web site development, parent relations, telephone etiquette and body language. Short-term goals are the response rates you expect from campaigns with a definite end-date, such as an open house, a summer program promotion or a community preschool fair. If you have committed to your long-term goals, your campaigns are more likely to meet with success.

The plan

A marketing plan should not be too complex, and the following outlines the components of an annual plan:

For a more detailed look at a marketing plan, complete with objectives, programs and calendar, see Appendix B

I. Executive Summary

This section is a summary of the entire plan and is easier to write last. Write a brief statement about each of the following sections to create a simple explanation of your marketing plan.

II. Current Situation

Include your business location, target market(s), competi-

tion and any additional issues that play a role in the decision making process regarding marketing.

III. Marketing Objectives

Identify your objectives and list them in simple language. What is it that you want to achieve with the marketing efforts outlined in this plan? How often do you intend to engage in marketing this year?

IV. Marketing Strategy

Describe what you offer and how you are going to communicate it to your target market. Include product/service description, pricing and payment details and promotional activities.

V. Action Programs

Highlight the basics of the promotional activities identified in the previous section. Each one only needs a brief explanation of what your plan is for implementing them.

VI. Budget

Building on the previous sections, the budget portion consists of actual dollar amounts. Each activity likely requires a certain amount of money to implement. List that information here, along with the grand total.

VII. Measurements

Similar to section III, the measurements should briefly state your goals in measurable language. This typically includes numbers and/or percentages. Measuring your goals helps you make decisions about your marketing activities.

VIII. Supporting Documents and Information

Depending on how detailed your plan is, you may choose

to include a calendar of your promotional activities, price quotes from vendors or lists of the publications you plan to contact for various efforts.

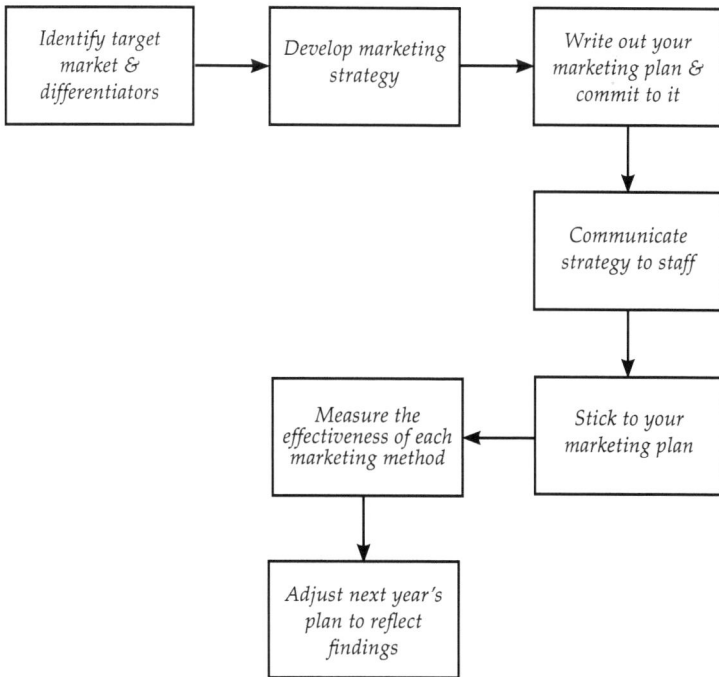

| Identify target market & differentiators | → | Develop marketing strategy | → | Write out your marketing plan & commit to it |

```
┌──────────────────┐      ┌──────────────────┐      ┌──────────────────┐
│ Identify target  │      │ Develop marketing│      │ Write out your   │
│   market &       │ ───▶ │    strategy      │ ───▶ │ marketing plan & │
│ differentiators  │      │                  │      │   commit to it   │
└──────────────────┘      └──────────────────┘      └──────────────────┘
                                                              │
                                                              ▼
                                                    ┌──────────────────┐
                                                    │  Communicate     │
                                                    │ strategy to staff│
                                                    └──────────────────┘
                                                              │
                                                              ▼
               ┌──────────────────┐              ┌──────────────────┐
               │  Measure the     │              │ Stick to your    │
               │effectiveness of  │ ◀─────────── │ marketing plan   │
               │ each marketing   │              │                  │
               │     method       │              └──────────────────┘
               └──────────────────┘
                        │
                        ▼
               ┌──────────────────┐
               │ Adjust next year's│
               │  plan to reflect  │
               │    findings       │
               └──────────────────┘
```

Understanding the basics steps to marketing is essential to creating a workable and realistic plan for your business. The above flowchart is a simple example of what you can follow when implementing your marketing plan.

Measuring the results

This step in the process is often overlooked, resulting in a marketing plan that suffers from a lack of feedback. If you do not know that 75% of your new business was a direct result of a single promotion and 0% came from your quarter-page advertisement, you will continue to waste a portion of your budget on the ad when a single text listing with your telephone number would be enough. Or, vice-versa: if 75% of your new business is a direct result of the ad, what are you spending the rest of your budget on? And is any of it working?

Use section five of your plan to create a matrix (see example) with space for names and campaigns. Print it off and post it by the telephone or in your office. As you receive phone calls, drop-ins and new customers, ask them how they heard about you.

You have the option of setting up a more elaborate tracking system, but a simple one works well for the first year or two. When you are ready, you can also begin tracking not only the efforts, but the process of the interaction with the prospect. You might want to know how many of your prospects call, then visit, and enroll in your program versus those who call, then visit, but do not enroll. Let's say that after one year of tracking this, you discover that 80% of prospects who visit your center do not enroll their children in your program. You could interpret this trend to mean that there is something disrupting the desired goal at that point in the process. By looking closely at how effective each marketing activity is, you can gather information to pinpoint necessary adjustments to your plan.

When asking someone how they heard about you, remember that people often forget entirely. They think it

Measurement Matrix

Family / Name	Telephone book listing	Resource & referral org.	Location (drove by)	Referral / Word of mouth	Open house	Flyer at local businesses	Other	Results
Jane Smith		✓						needs infant care; referred to other provider
Alvarez family				✓				enrolled one child
			✓					
				✓				
			✓					
			✓					
		✓						
							✓	
			✓					
			✓					
					✓			
				✓				
					✓			
			✓					
				✓				
					✓			
TOTALS	0	2	6	4	3	0	1	

was an ad in the telephone book, but it was really your involvement in a community event. Even though your statistics may not be 100% accurate, your annual tally should paint a picture of what is and is not working for you.

Tally up the results from your matrix every six months and begin to think about your plan for the next year. If you find that you have a lot of drive-by traffic, take advantage of your new knowledge to appeal to more people driving by. Catch their attention by adding a bouquet of balloons to your mailbox every Monday morning. If you have mostly referrals, make it even easier for people to tell others about you by printing referral cards or creating a web site and developing an email campaign.

Ready to start

As you have surely figured out by now, participating in marketing is not optional. Because it envelops everything you do and sends a message about who you are, you must take control of what message you are sending and manage your marketing with a budget and a plan. Remember the four rules and continue learning about how to create and implement successful marketing campaigns.

You must COMMIT to your marketing plan and not waver.

You must provide CONSISTENCY among all marketing efforts.

You must regard marketing as a long-term INVESTMENT.

You must have PATIENCE.

When faced with the decision of whether or not to take a risk, remember that you cannot expect extraordinary results from ordinary marketing efforts. Bring in a professional to train your faculty on parent relations, support the community through interesting and unusual methods or offer your customers something they cannot get anywhere else.

The true investment of marketing is time and effort. The costs associated with it are as varied as the efforts you choose to implement. Again, you rarely see a return on your marketing dollars immediately. It takes time to see the results of your marketing activities, but if you maintain a commitment to your plan, your wait will not be as long as if you were starting from scratch. Maintenance is much easier than struggling with a new plan every time enrollment is low.

Understanding what marketing is and how to apply specific knowledge is beneficial to the success of your business, but never forget that running a high-quality center with well-trained and caring faculty members is one of the best ways to consistently obtain referrals and positive word-of-mouth, keeping your program full of students.

Chapter Eight

Scenarios to Consider

Every situation is unique and the following scenarios may not apply to your specific marketing needs. However, use them as guides to develop solutions for your own business and organizational issues. Read each scenario and, before turning the page, compare it to a similar situation you face. Based on what you have learned and what you already know from experience, decide which marketing techniques you would apply.

Scenario one

You opened your center a year ago, but business is still slow. You have a sign outside, a listing in the yellow pages and a very small budget. You need to create interest quickly. What are some ways you can do that?

Scenario one

- First, you need to determine what *is* working for you: your location? your sign? word-of-mouth?

  Is your sign helping or hurting you? (see Chapter 3)

  Are you getting any business from your yellow pages listing? If not, how much is it costing you?

- If your current families are happy with your service, start a referral program.

- Run a promotion.

- Hold an event specific to caring for young children and call the newspaper.

- Give brochures to local schools, real estate agents, pediatricians, and other local businesses to distribute.

- Change your services and communicate the changes with flyers, a press release to local paper, and conversation with parents.

Scenario two

A parent enrolls their child in your program. During that first week you _____.

Scenario two

- Send home a "First Day of School" card with a photo* of the child.
- Send home a detailed note on the last day of week.
- Email an update to the parent at work.
- Make sure the environment is ready: Name on cubby, name on "go home" box, photo on the "I am here" board.
- Email a digital photo of the child to his or her parent at work.
- Do something special for the entire class on a new student's first day or week: offer a special treat or lunch, let everyone wear special hats, decorate the classroom, etc.
- Post photos on bulletin board of the children welcoming new students.

*be sure you have obtained all necessary release forms

Scenario three

You have decided to hold a special afternoon of messy finger painting with the local senior center. All permission slips and photo release forms are in, and participants are bringing appropriate clothing for the event. You have two weeks to promote this event with the message that your center is fun and provides high quality of care. You decide that telling the community about what you are doing is the most effective marketing at this time. How do you intend to communicate your message to the public?

Scenario three

BEFORE

- Invite the local press to attend the event.
- Put a notice about it on your web site.
- Post information on your bulletin board.
- Invite families to observe or help.
- Advertise the event in your newsletter.
- Send out announcement postcards to families.
- Co-market with the senior center.

AFTER

- Document it on your web site with photos, a story, and quotes from the participants.
- Send home artwork.
- Post artwork in entry hall.
- Email photos to parents.
- Put a photo on shirts and distribute to children.
- Document the event in your newsletter.
- Send a postcard with details of the event to all addresses in your zip code.
- Issue a press release on the success of the event, with quotes from the children and seniors.

Scenario four

You and your faculty just finished several hours of training, bringing everyone beyond the minimum requirements for your state. How can you use that wise decision to further your marketing efforts?

Scenario four

- Post announcement on bulletin board.
- Hold a "Meet the Teachers" event and encourage faculty to share new information on relevant topics for your families.
- List the names of trainees and trainings in your newsletter.
- List the names of trainees and trainings on your web site.
- Create a promotional piece that highlights the benefits to families when faculty is trained.
- Make sure your well-trained faculty is mentioned on your web site and brochure.
- Encourage faculty to share their knowledge with families.
- Send out a press release to your local paper.
- Reward faculty for taking their career seriously.
- Post training details or handouts in center.

Scenario five

You have decided that a referral program will best serve your current marketing goals. What are your options for implementing the program? What do you need? Who gets to participate in the program? How do you determine from whom the reference came? What is the reward/incentive? Are you going to publish or track the results?

Scenario five

Document the plan in writing and share the details with participants. You should have something participants can hand out: card, flyer, etc. Also, determine if you want to include faculty, families or both.

Set the rules/guidelines:

Must the referred person enroll their child in order to obtain the reward or does the referred person have to visit the center for a tour?

You must provide an easy method for both referring and referred parties to participate. The creation of a card with your phone number, address and a place for the referring person's name is a helpful tool.

Establish a reward/incentive:

If the reward is of value to the receiver, you will probably get higher participation.

Families: 10% off one month for both families when enrollment occurs or $25 gift certificate for the referring family.

Faculty: One day off for every enrolled child, $5 coffee card for every two walk-ins or $25 gift certificate for each enrolled child.

Adjusting to factors beyond your control

An annual art auction and raffle proved to be a successful fundraiser for one childcare center many years in a row. Local businesses donated items for the raffle and an art gallery gave the center materials to frame artwork created by the children at the center. These completed pieces were then auctioned at the annual fundraiser.

After years of great success, a slowing economy forced those businesses to cancel donations and the gallery had to close its doors. The school needed to raise funds, but faced a lack of support and immediate ideas. The faculty gathered to brainstorm. Since businesses were unable to assist, they concluded that a family-based event with donated personal hours from themselves was their best option. Instead of giving up or continuing with an event that was not serving the needs of the center, this school evaluated their situation and the positive results from the previous years to create a foundation for the new event.

The original art auction and raffle morphed into a family carnival, complete with inflatable bouncing structures, dunk tank, silent auction, relevant vendors and several games for children of all ages. Each activity "costs" a certain amount of tickets, so participants purchase reasonably priced tickets from staff volunteers. The games and activities are a huge hit with families, and the number of attendees grows larger every year. Using donations, staff support, keen negotiation skills and parent participation, the carnival profits $2000 annually and enrolls new students year after year.

Appendix A

Resources

GENERAL MARKETING

Guerilla Marketing, by Jay Conrad Levinson

Program Full: 100 Ideas to Promote Your Childcare Business, by Taffy Gallagher (coming soon - Summer 2006)

marketingprofs.com

PROFESSIONALISM

The Visionary Director: A Handbook for Dreaming, Organizing, and Improvising in Your Center, by Margie Carter, Deb Curtis

Professionalism is for Everyone: Five Keys to Being a True Professional, by James R. Ball

True Professionalism, by David H. Maister

Reading People: How to Understand People and Predict Their Behavior--Anytime, Anyplace, by Jo-Ellan Dimitrius, Mark C. Mazzarella

Teach Yourself Body Language, by Gordon Wainright

Body Language, by Julius Fast

Understanding Body Language (Barron's Business Success Series), by Geoff Ribbens, Richard Thompson

Visible Thoughts: The New Psychology of Body Language, by Geoffrey Beattie

Gestures: The Do's and Taboos of Body Language Around the World, by Roger E. Axtell, Mike Fornwald

The following are books written for parents that you may find useful in determining what your strengths and objectives are:

The Unofficial Guide to Childcare, by Ann Douglas

The Anxious Parents' Guide to Quality Childcare, by Michelle Ehrich

PROFESSIONAL DEVELOPMENT

National Association for the Education of Young Children (NAEYC): naeyc.org (*Young Children,* NAEYC Journal: journal.naeyc.org)

Educational Training Partners: educationaltraining-partners.org (*Early Years Review,* newsletter: visit above web site)

National Association for Family Child Care: nafcc.org

National Child Care Information Center: nccic.org

Child Care Information Exchange: childcareexchange.com (*250 Management Success Stories from Childcare Directors,* Child Care Information Exchange)

National Network for Child Care: nncc.org

DESIGN

General:

Basics of Design: Layout and Typography for Beginners, by Lisa Graham

mydesignprimer.com

Color: colormatters.com, pantone.com

Stock images: creatas.com, comstock.com, corbis.com, gettyimages.com, punchstock.com

Printing: free or inexpensive business card resources:

vistaprint.com, dcp-print.com

printingforless.com (SAVE $25.00 off your first order when you use the referral code: RP1SF5QX)

Web search terms: graphic design guidelines, desktop publishing basics, color and design, using photos in design, low cost printing, digital printing guide, offset printing, printing marketing collateral at home

GRAMMAR, PUNCTUATION, SPELLING

Webster's New World Dictionary

Webster's New World Thesaurus

Webster's New World Guide to Punctuation: All the rules you need to know to punctuate correctly

The Well-Tempered Sentence: A Punctuation Handbook for the Innocent, the Eager, and the Doomed, by Karen Elizabeth Gordon

The American Heritage Dictionary, 4th edition

bartleby.com   m-w.com

PUBLIC RELATIONS

The Public Relations Writer's Handbook, by Merry Aronson and Don Spetner

Web search terms: small business press release, writing your own press release, how to write a press release, getting noticed by the media, creating media buzz for small businesses

DIRECT MAIL

The Direct Marketing Association: <u>dma.org</u>

United States Postal Service: <u>usps.com</u>

Web search terms: direct mail design tips, direct mail response rates, direct mail

WEB SITE

Hosting: Verio® (verio.com), Speakeasy® (speakeasy.net), WorkZ Sites® (workzsites.com), Volusion® (volusion.com), Yahoo® (yahoo.com)

Learning Web Design, by Jennifer Niederst

BUDGET

Marketing on a Shoestring, by J. Davidson

Appendix B

Sample Marketing Plan

Note: All information in this sample plan is fictional.

I. Executive Summary

ABC Childcare Center is a licensed childcare facility serving children ages 18 mos. to 5 yrs. and is owned and operated by Taffy Gallagher. The company cares for children of families living and working in the area south of Seattle, WA.

Our particular location attracts families of varying income and ethnic backgrounds. We have eight faculty members, two with language skills in Spanish and Vietnamese, allowing for a wider range of literacy options, language development and cultural relevance.

We recently extended our hours from 6:30 AM – 5:30 PM to 6:00 AM – 6:00 PM. We also offer prepared meals, developmentally appropriate curriculum and two field trips per month. Our center is accredited by the National Association for the Education of Young Children, and all of our faculty members have their CDA, Bachelor degree, or 6+ years of relevant experience. We also pay for on-site training for our faculty on a wide range of topics.

The competition consists of three other agencies selling similar services to families in the immediate area. A brief exploration into a select number of competitor web sites and brochures reveals a lack of early hours, prepared meals and well-trained faculty. ABC Childcare possesses the capability of increasing our professional edge based on these three differentiators. All promotional activity should direct prospects to call us to schedule a visit.

For the upcoming year, a comprehensive marketing strategy includes faculty training, press releases, web site development, referral program, a new outdoor sign and a promotion that results in publicity for ABC Childcare.

ABC's management team consists of Taffy Gallagher, Director and Jane Doe, Assistant Director.

II. Current Situation

Location: ABC Childcare Center is located at 100 Main St. in Seattle, WA.

Target Markets

Primary market: Local families / parents with children age 18 mos. – 5 yrs.

Secondary market: Commuting parents with children age 18 mos. – 5 yrs.

Clients identify themselves as: busy, caring, educated, overworked, underpaid, doing their best

Competition

123 Daycare

Strengths: Very visible location, large sign, playground visible from street

Weaknesses: They don't take children under 2 yrs.

Address: 123 Main St.

Phone: 123-456-7890

Web site: 123daycare.com

XYZ Center

Strengths: Great web site, take payments online, well-qualified faculty

Weaknesses: Monthly fees are 20% higher than ours

Address: 555 W. Main St.

Phone: 123-555-1212

Web site: xyzcenter.com

A1 Preschool

Strengths: Interesting location in nice building, easy access to parking

Weaknesses: They operate on limited hours (9-11:30 AM and 2:30-5 PM)

Address: 123 E. Main St.

Phone: 098-756-4321

Web site: A1preschool.com

<u>Issues</u>

Road construction during the spring may restrict access to our back parking lot.

Maternity leave for two teachers is occurring this year.

III. Marketing Objectives

Increase awareness of ABC Childcare Center's new hours among target audience.

Increase awareness of ABC Childcare Center's new hours among secondary audience.

Engage in a minimum of three marketing efforts each month.

IV. Marketing Strategy

The general method for increasing the amount of prospects looking to us for service is by clearly and consistently communicating our differentiators using our web site, press releases, outdoor sign and word-of-mouth.

The general method for obtaining referrals from current

customers is by providing professional high-quality service and well-trained faculty.

Service description

ABC Childcare Center is a licensed childcare facility serving ages 18 mos. to 5 yrs. The company provides education for families in the Seattle area. We offer full- and half-day programs that focus on both developmentally appropriate curriculum as well as school readiness. Our philosophy leans toward creating an open, welcoming and natural environment where children can explore their own learning styles with observation and guidance from our highly-trained staff members.

Our particular location attracts families of varying income and ethnic backgrounds, allowing for rich diversity and cultural awareness. We have eight faculty members, two with language skills in Spanish and Vietnamese, giving us a wider range of literacy options, language development and cultural relevance.

We recently extended our hours from 7:00 AM - 6:00 PM to 6:00 AM - 6:30 PM and will assess the impact of this change at three month intervals. We also offer prepared meals, developmentally appropriate curriculum and two **field trips per month. Our center is accredited by the** National Association for the Education of Young Children and three of our faculty members have their CDA. We also offer one-hour parent education classes every other Tuesday.

Pricing and payment options

$700.00 — Per child per month (Single-child family)

$650.00 — Per child per month (Two-child family)

$600.00 — Per child per month (Three or more children)

Cash and checks are the only acceptable forms of payment.

Purchasers receive a receipt confirmation and a hand-written thank you card via mail within one week.

Promotional activities
> Web site development
> Press releases
> Faculty training
> New outdoor sign
> Monday Mudday Promo
> Customer service
> Referral program

V. Action Programs

Web site development

Develop a 5-8 page web site highlighting our strengths, services and differentiators: licensed center, qualified faculty, extended hours, national accreditation, field trips, happy client testimonials.

Press releases

Three to five announcements for major changes to service, exceptional training accomplishments, Monday Mudday and any additional newsworthy topics that arise.

Faculty training

Deliver two hours faculty training each month on topics of relevance: environments, professionalism, guidance, customer service, literacy, special needs, sensory, and other topics to be determined.

New outdoor sign

Replace outdoor sign with large, long-lasting sign.

Monday MudDay Promo

Create outdoor mud area for children to play in. Develop games focused on sensory education and invite the local media to attend. Highlight the benefits of teaching children in this manner and encourage families to participate. Ask everyone to bring old clothing and a change of clothes.

Customer service (mail)

Mail hand-written thank you cards with receipts. Train faculty on customer service and professionalism. Keep extended hours available for a minimum of one year to measure response.

Referral program

Create a referral program that makes it easy (and worthwhile) for teachers and families to refer other families to our center.

Next year's action programs

All of the above that worked

Local movie theater advertising

Partnership with senior center

Resource and Referral listing

VI. Budget

TOTAL MARKETING BUDGET = $ 8,000.00

Web site hosting package = $299.88
$24.99 per month

Faculty training = $2,000.00
10 mos. @ $200 per month

New outdoor sign = $565.00

MudDay promo = $800.00
Flyer printing = $150
Hoses and swimming pools = $250
Decorations and food = $100

Customer service (mail) = $300
Note Cards = $50
Postage = $100
Discretionary = $150

Referral program = $500
Gift cards/certificates = $300
Printing = $150
Measurement poster = $50

VII. Measurements

Increase enrollment by 20% in 12 months: 10 new enrollees.

Net sales of approximately $1,800.00 per month

Average new students per month: .83

Average new students per week: .19

VIII. Supporting Documents and Information

• Promotion activities calendar (see next page)

• Faculty training fee proposal (attach proposal to plan)

• $2,000.00 for ten hours of all-faculty training on environments, professionalism, guidance, customer service, literacy, special needs, sensory, and other topics to be determined.

• New outdoor sign quote: $565.00 for 4' x 6' sign.

ANNUAL MARKETING CALENDAR

JANUARY	Web site development Press release for new hours Faculty training Customer service: thank you notes and telephone etiquette
FEBRUARY	Web site development Faculty training Customer service: thank you notes and dress/grooming
MARCH	Launch web site Faculty training Customer service: thank you notes and telephone etiquette Assess change of hours impact
APRIL	Web site development Faculty training Customer service: thank you notes and body language
MAY	Faculty training Customer service: thank you notes and body language MudDay prep work: write release, prepare flyers, purchase supplies Update web site New outdoor sign installation
JUNE	Press release for MudDay Monday MudDay promotion Customer service: thank you notes Assess change of hours impact

JULY	Referral program prep work Faculty training Customer service: thank you notes
AUGUST	Launch referral program Faculty training Customer service: thank you notes
SEPTEMBER	Update web site Assess change of hours impact Faculty training Customer service: thank you notes Awards for referral program
OCTOBER	Faculty training Customer service: thank you notes Awards for referral program
NOVEMBER	Faculty training Customer service: thank you notes Awards for referral program
DECEMBER	Update web site Customer service: thank you notes Assess change of hours impact Awards for referral program

About the Author

Taffy Gallagher is the owner of a marketing company special-izing in services for non-profit and small business firms. She has been engaged in the leadership of several organizations including Educational Training Partners, the Chinook Tribe of Washington State, Five Threads, and the Childhood Matters Conference. After years of conducting marketing-oriented workshops for the child-care and early learning communities, she recognized a need for a convenient, inexpensive and easily accessible version of those workshops. This book is the result of that need.

**Don't miss the newest marketing book
for the childcare and early learning communities**

100 Ideas to Market Your Childcare Business

by Taffy Gallagher

A list of over 100 ideas to help you market your center or program. Building on the foundation of Program Full: Your Guide to Successful Childcare Marketing, you will get promotional campaign ideas and simple marketing tips to get your program noticed.

Place your order at saltwaterzapf.com.

15459868R00079

Made in the USA
Lexington, KY
29 May 2012